Jesus Asked.

Jesus Asked.
What He Wanted to Know

CoNRaD GeMPf

ZONDERVAN™

GRAND RAPIDS, MICHIGAN 49530 USA

ZONDERVAN™

Jesus Asked.
Copyright © 2003 by Conrad Gempf

Requests for information should be addressed to:
Zondervan, *Grand Rapids, Michigan 49530*

Library of Congress Cataloging-in-Publication Data

Gempf, Conrad
    Jesus asked : what he wanted to know / Conrad Gempf.
        p. cm.
    Includes index.
    ISBN 0-310-24773-X
    1. Jesus Christ—Conversations. 2. Questioning in the Bible.
    I. Title.
 BT306 .G46 2003
 232.9'5—dc21
                                                    2002014449
                                                        CIP

Interior design by Susan Ambs

Printed in the United Kingdom

---

02 03 04 05 06 07/❖ CLY/ 10 9 8 7 6 5 4 3 2 1

in memory of
Alfons and Dorothy Gempf,
my parents,
themselves inquisitive people, full of wonder

Contents

Always Asking
Questions

I wanna ask ya somethin'.

Asking and Telling

Clark "Superman" Kent suffered from two weaknesses that didn't plague Jesus or my childhood friend Richie: (1) Kryptonite and (2) Bad Dialogue.

Dialogue might be an odd thing to remember about Richie, but that's how it was. He may have been the youngest of the four of us who hung out together, but he was never one to be trifled with. Richie was a drummer and even had a drum set in his basement—something too cool for words. But he also had a peculiar way of getting your attention.

Here's the scene: Brian and I would be discussing something Richie didn't care about, perhaps which trading card was The Best or what sports car could go the fastest. If he wanted to change the subject, he didn't ask, "Hey, can we talk about something else?" Nor did he settle for the even more involving "You know what?" Instead he would employ a special gambit. Thirty-odd years later, I can still remember him looking at me earnestly and saying, "Conrad, I wanna ask ya somethin'."

As a rhetorical tactic, this was worthy of the ancient orators. I can easily imagine Demosthenes and Cicero congratulating Richie. For it is relatively simple to resist a change to the subject by means of "Can we talk about something else?"—especially when the would-be conversational hijacker is smaller than you. And the otherwise intriguing "You know what?" was bait I could steer clear of. But it took me a surprisingly long time to wise up to Richie's trick. Even the most subtle and complex debates about who was cooler, Bond or the men from U.N.C.L.E., wound up ceding the conversational playing field to Richie's "I wanna ask ya somethin'."

The power and brilliance of this tactic comes from the tantalizing promise it extends. Richie implicitly commits himself to seize the spotlight in order to give it back. I may be speaking now, but here is an opportunity to hold the floor again, and this time with an audience all the more keen to hear what I have to say. For the "ask ya somethin'" cocktail also contains implied flattery: My point of view on the matter is of interest. "You know what?" fails because I must admit ignorance and then listen to some pronouncement, but "I wanna ask ya somethin'" is an invitation for *me* to pronounce judgment. And in those days, Brian, Clifford, and I were nothing if not full of verdicts waiting to be delivered.

But now I must expose Richie to the world. For he was sublimely clever (some would say insidious) because he never actually had any question in mind. What would follow his "I wanna ask ya somethin'" would be some detailed description of what happens if a dentist drills too far inside of your tooth or some story starring a friend of a cousin who had a close brush with death in the form of a postal worker with one too many snowball marks on his sack.

And yet I would follow all these proceedings with great care, not wishing to miss any detail lest that prove the very point about which my considered opinion was requested. But fifteen or twenty minutes later, Richie would be done with his story, my mother would be calling me, and the conversation would have ground to a halt, having been irretrievably subverted. And all without anything remotely like a question ever having come to his lips.

Jesus, as best we can judge from the surviving historical records, almost certainly did not have a drum set in his basement. But he is similar to my friend Richie in this other business. At the Olympic level of sprint, intermediate, and long-distance Conversation Hijacking, not even Richie would have a chance against Jesus. But unlike Richie, Jesus actually *did* get around to asking the questions. In fact, one of the most surprising things about the gospels is that they report Jesus as asking questions more often than not.

The Greatest Teacher . . . Not?

Long before I noticed the question-wielding habit of Jesus, I was speaking to a group and going out of my way to avoid controversy when bringing up the subject of him. I gently began with the cliché I'd heard countless others say: "Of course, everyone agrees that Jesus was one of the greatest teachers who ever lived." If you've heard this pronouncement by those countless others, you'll note my concession in saying "one of the greatest." But I still didn't get away with it. I expected everyone to nod, thinking to themselves, *Yes, yes, get on with it. . . .* Instead, the guy in the leather jacket objected.

"I'm not saying that Jesus wasn't a good person and all that, okay?" he began. "But I can't see how he can be called one of greatest teachers who ever lived."

I stared at him, clearly not understanding his objections.

"Well," he explained, "there really isn't that much that he taught us, is there? And in the end he didn't convince that many people—only about a dozen." He shrugged.

I hardly knew how to continue. I scrambled and came up with something about the delayed effects of his teaching and the way the Jesus movement became so influential all around the planet. But deep down I knew that the guy was right: It was possible, even tempting, to consider Jesus as an ineffective teacher in his own lifetime. At least it is if we don't think too carefully about the standards by which teachers should be evaluated.

It seems as though a truly great teacher should have a vast store of knowledge and should be able to communicate it clearly and with an air of persuasive authority. I'd always unthinkingly placed Jesus in this category. But, let's face it, he doesn't seem to fit that mold. Although the gospels frequently mention that people noticed his air of authority, it is much less common for them to report that people were actually becoming convinced of what he said. The first-century Pharisees appreciated a good argument. Jesus rarely gave them one, and even more rarely persuaded them of anything.

So this objection from the floor troubled me a great deal. If Jesus were sent from God, if he were anything like what Christians have claimed him to be, surely he could have been a better communicator than he was! Instead, his teaching was often misunderstood even by his own intimate band of followers, sometimes to the point that they complained to him about it.

But even more peculiar, as I reread my gospels I noticed that they didn't portray Jesus as being incredibly smart or knowledgeable. We don't find any mathematical or scientific revelations from his lips. In fact, the gospels seem to go out of their way to present a Jesus who asks questions and who, in at least one notable case, doesn't know the answers of questions addressed to him.

What Jesus Didn't Know

There's something he doesn't know?! Well, actually, yes, the gospel of Mark recounts a time when Jesus admits it. To understand how remarkable this is, though, we need to hit the Ancient History Rewind button. In Jesus' day, many religious people thought that the events of their day heralded the end of the universe. Borrowing imagery from the Old Testament prophets, such as Ezekiel and Daniel, they wrote books of visions and predictions about the heavens and how beasts would ravage the earth. These writings primarily sought to put the coming horrors and chaos into perspective: After a definite measure of time, the Lord would assert his authority with a definitive cosmic clobbering. Evil might appear to be making short-term gains, but God's eventual triumph was sure and certain. We could say that the motto of these books is Don't Panic! They were the self-help or management consultant books of their day and their authors were the gurus.

Against this backdrop of apocalyptic expectations, it is no wonder that Jesus' disciples hope for some direction from *their* spiritual teacher. And when Jesus predicts a catastrophic future event—the destruction of the Jerusalem Temple—the disciples begin to draw up their own timetables for the coming cataclysms and triumphs (see Mark 13). They ask him, "When will these things happen? And what will be the sign that they are all about to be fulfilled?" (Matthew clarifies this question as: "Tell us, when will this happen and what will be the sign of your coming and of the end of the age?")

But here is where the surprise comes. I guarantee that no contemporary evangelical Christian or skeptical scholar would compose for Jesus the reply that the gospel's Jesus actually gives. The Mark 13 speech starts with just the kind of thing the disciples would expect: wars and rumors of wars. You can almost hear the *scritch-scritch* of the disciples' pencils against their notebooks as they try to get all this good end-time teaching down. But then Jesus breaks the spell and says, matter of factly, "but the end is not yet." Oh dear, turn the pencils over and rub it all out.

Then just when he seems to get back on the right track, speaking of nation against nation, earthquakes, and famines, he does it again: "This is but the *beginning* of birth pangs."

You can almost hear Peter interjecting, "Are you going to give us a timetable of the end times or not?" If he had asked, Jesus' answer would surely have been "Not." Clearly he was not terribly interested in telling them what they wanted to know. They wanted to know what to look for; he wanted to tell them how to be looking. That's why his subject shifts from things to watch for to his command to watch out and be alert.

The central paradox, and the main point for our purposes, comes when Jesus begins the second major part of the speech (Mark 13:28–31). He says that by watching you will be able to tell, as with the fig tree, when the time is ripe. But then in verse 32 he says that you will never know the timing of the event in advance and that *he himself does not know* when it will happen.

How this must have surprised the disciples: The day and time have been set and the Father knows it already, but Jesus does not! Imagine how hard this must have been for the early Christians to accept and write into one of their foundational documents. Jesus, who knew people's hearts, who is on such intimate terms with the Father, who should be in control of all things, not only refuses to tell his disciples something that other religious teachers happily tell their followers, but even admits his ignorance on the subject.

Some contemporary Christians will find this gospel passage disturbing as well. But it cuts two ways. Although it says something about Jesus Christ that is difficult for believers, it also says something very difficult to unbelievers. The gospel of Mark, at least, is not propaganda, merely reciting the "party line" about Jesus or creating fictional stories to show Jesus in the best possible light in all situations. The very fact that the gospels are sometimes difficult for Christians points to their integrity. They haven't been written just to make Christianity easy.

What we learn in Mark 13 coheres with other parts of the New Testament. When trying to encourage humility and fellowship in one of his congregations, Paul either writes or quotes a hymn about what Jesus gave up to become human (Phil. 2:5–11). It is easy to believe that an intimate knowledge of the universe would have been among the things that Jesus gave up. It looks as though he gave up omniscience (knowledge of everything) along with omnipresence (being everywhere at once). Perhaps it is impossible to be like us and also know the universe that way.

But if Jesus was not born knowing everything, this implies that he could be taught. And if what we've said is true, it's even likely that the Lord would have scored less than 100 percent when someone tested him about something that he hadn't yet learned. (Ignorance is no excuse for doing something wrong, but it is not a sin in itself.)

Jesus and His Teachers

But how presumptuous of anyone to give Jesus something like a spelling test! The medieval Christians clearly felt the sting of such apparent irreverence when one of them wrote a piece called *The Infancy Gospel of Thomas*. Not to be confused with the earlier, more dangerous *Gnostic Gospel of Thomas*, one should regard the *Infancy Gospel* as on the same level as a contemporary children's storybook titled *Everyday Life in Jesus' Village*. Unfortunately, this fictional work owes more to the writer's imagination and the ideas of the time than it does to first-century history or, probably, to Jesus' own life.

We learn in the *Infancy Gospel* that as a lad Jesus is clearly powerful, though very much a boy and often barely aware of his own strength. For instance, once, when playing on a roof, Jesus accidentally causes his buddy to fall to his death. All is not lost, however, for Jesus simply brings him back to life again. Or on another occasion, the artistic boy Jesus made some lovely models of birds from lumps of clay, then clapped his hands to turn them into real birds, which took flight immediately.

These tales often stand in marked contrast to the real gospel stories, perhaps none more so than the *Infancy Gospel*'s story of the man who wanted to teach Jesus the alphabet.

A certain teacher, Zacchaeus by name, heard Jesus talking and was astonished that a child could say such things. And after a few days he came to Joseph and said to him, "You have a clever child with great understanding. Come, hand him over to me so that he may learn letters." ... And so Zacchaeus told him all the letters from Alpha to Omega distinctly and with some questioning. But Jesus looked at him and said, "How is it that you, who do not yet really know the essence of Alpha, teach others Beta? Hypocrite! First, if you know it, teach the meaning of the Alpha, and then we will be ready to believe you about Beta!" Then he began to quiz the teacher about the first letter, and the teacher was unable to answer the questions. And then in front of all of them, the child said to the teacher, "Hear then, teacher, the arrangement of the first letter, and notice how it has lines and a middle stroke which goes through the lines which you see, and how these lines converge, rise, and turn in the dance, three signs of the same kind, subject to and supporting one another, of equal proportions. Here you have the lines of the Alpha."

Now when Zacchaeus the teacher heard many such allegorical descriptions of the first letter being expounded by the child, he was perplexed at such a reply and said to those who were there, "Woe is me, I have brought shame to myself in trying to be teacher over such a child: this child is not of earth—he can even subdue fire; perhaps he was from before the beginning of the world. I cannot attain his level of understanding. I have deceived myself, thrice wretched man that I am. I wanted to take on a pupil, and have found I have a teacher. Therefore I beg you, brother Joseph, take him back to your house. Whatever great thing he is, a god or an angel, I do not know."

The contrast between this tale and the only genuine story we have about Jesus' boyhood could hardly be more stark. And it couldn't be easier to tell which one is fiction and which is history. We learn in the second chapter of Luke's gospel that the boy Jesus gets lost. The family is heading for home and he somehow stays behind. When his parents go back to find him, he is in the Temple. Doing what? "After three days they found him in the temple courts, sitting among the teachers, listen to them and asking them questions" (Luke 2:46). It's true that the next verse tells us that all who heard him were astonished by his understanding and his replies, but that should not deflect us from the amazing first statement that the person whom the gospel writer believed to be the fulfillment of the Law and the Prophets came to the Temple on this occasion with an attitude of listening and asking questions.

This habit of asking questions appears to have stayed with Jesus all his life. In the first gospel to have been written, the gospel of Mark, there are 67 episodes in which there is any sort of conversation at all. Even when you are careful to count double questions as one—"Whose face is that on the coin? Whose inscription is it printed with?"—we have 50 questions of Jesus in those 67 episodes. And the pattern seems to hold throughout the gospels.

Jesus was a bit different from other religious teachers. Moses wanted to tell you the Law of God. Prophets were always telling you what the Lord was saying. But apparently if you met Jesus on the street, he was more likely to ask you something than to tell you something. Even when other people asked him a question, he often replied with one of his own.

Question: Good teacher, what must I do to inherit eternal life?

Response: Why do you call me good?

Question: Is it lawful to pay taxes to Caesar or not?

Response: Whose picture is on the coin?

Question: For what grounds should divorce be permitted?

Response: What does Moses command you?

Question: By what authority do you do these things?

Response: Answer me this, by what authority did John the Baptist do what he did?

Questions and more questions.

The Journey Ahead of Us

We have seen in this introduction how my old friend Richie taught me the real power of even threatening to ask a question. From my leather-clad objector, I learned that Jesus may not have been the Great Teacher that I thought he was—at least not the way that I reckoned greatness in teachers. And the gospels show us that Jesus is not the superhuman repository of all knowledge that some might expect. Instead, we find a Jesus who admits ignorance and who asks questions. A whole lot of questions.

In the chapters that follow, we'll zoom through the four gospels and I'll be your tour guide, stopping the tour-camel for you to disembark and explore various points of interest. You'll see that sometimes the questions that Jesus asked have very simple answers. Sometimes he seems to have used questions in order to avoid issues, but in other occasions he used questions as a surgical strike to the command and control center of a problem. And it isn't just the "bad guys" who are on the receiving end of his blunt and difficult questions; we'll see the disciples saved from a storm only to be blown away by a verbal barrage.

Before we're done, you'll see Jesus asking very difficult questions that have no obvious answer, notably the apostle

Peter's mid-term exam. On one of our tour stops, you'll see Jesus "pulling the legs" of a couple of disciples (the Greek text actually says that he "pretends").

We'll finish up by considering the most effective ways to avoid answering Jesus' questions using New Testament evaders as our role models and by reconsidering the larger, overarching question of what it was that he wanted to know.

Before all of that, though, we need to have a quick look at another feature of Jesus' teaching. When he wasn't asking questions, he was telling story-shaped riddles, which are a type of question. We call them parables.

Chapter One

Constantly Speaking In Riddles

Can the blind lead the blind?

What Is a "Parable"?

As I hope I've demonstrated in the introduction, nothing was more characteristic of Jesus' speaking than the fact that he constantly asked questions. Most people, even people who write about Jesus, don't seem to have picked that up. But almost everyone *has* noticed a facet of Jesus' teaching style that is closely related to his questions: he often taught in parables. To see the connection between parable and question, we have to look under the surface.

For most folks, it's a parable if it's a story with a message. Once upon a time there was a vineyard owner with three sons who cast out their nets and caught wheat as well as tares. And the landlord returned in the middle of the night and said to the Samaritan who had sold everything he had in order to buy the pearl, "You have forgiven much so much will be forgiven you," but to the one who buried his talents and had no oil in his lamp he said, "Depart from me, I never knew you, and kill the fatted calf on your way out." Or something like that. Now that's a parable!

For Jesus and the people of his time, though, you didn't need the plot, dialogue, or multiple characters in order for something to be shelved in the Parable aisle at Turns-of-Phrase-R-Us. Their conception of parable included a good deal more than ours. A first-century person would use the term *parable* any time someone talked about a subject figuratively. Stories like the Prodigal Son or Lost Sheep fit the bill, but so do such sentence-length stories as: "He told them still another parable: 'The kingdom of heaven is like yeast that a woman took and mixed into about eighteen pounds of flour until it worked all through the dough'" (Matt. 13:33) or "Can the blind lead the blind? Will they not both fall into a pit?" (Luke 6:39).

In fact, on one occasion, Jesus called a mere phrase a parable. In Luke 4:23, he says to the people of the synagogue, "Surely you will quote this parable to me: 'Physician, heal yourself.'" Three words. Yet it's a parable. The translators knew you and I wouldn't think of it as a parable so they translated it "proverb," but the Greek word is parable: *parabolē.*

The word that I've used in the chapter title, *riddle,* is a similar word. Nowadays when we use that word we almost always mean a joke of the form "question with trick answer": What's orange and sounds like a parrot? A carrot.

But we also recognize the term as used for a longer puzzle with a trick answer. An example of this kind of riddle is the old conundrum:

> *As I was going to St. Ives,*
> *I met a man with seven wives.*
> *Each wife had seven sacks,*
> *each sack had seven cats,*
> *each cat had seven kits.*
> *Kits, cats, sacks, and wives—*
> *how many were going to St. Ives?*

The answer is one. The polygamist and his feline crew were traveling in the opposite direction; only the narrator was going to St. Ives. Another example, a riddle from the ancient world, is the Greek legend that the Sphinx asked Oedipus: What is the creature that walks on four legs in the morning, two legs at noon, and three in the evening? The answer is man, who crawls as a baby, walks tall through most of his life, and then uses a cane in old age.

A riddle is, then, a figure of speech that wants some figuring out, usually by lateral thinking. And this is exactly what's going on in Jesus' parables. But in Jesus' case, they are not mere jokes or puzzles and not only told for their entertainment value. They are told to make a point—to teach—but they might do so in this roundabout sideways-thinking way. They may even do something more than that; we'll see about that later.

Making It Easy?

Mrs. Bayster, my Sunday school teacher, always told us that Jesus spoke in parables for a very simple reason. He wanted to teach some fairly complex theological concepts (these are not Mrs. Bayster's precise words) to people who, unfortunately, did not have the benefit of the weekly Sunday school and were not well enough educated to understand a straight-forward technical discussion. Thus, the theory goes, he wrapped up these theological truths in story form. Plain folks couldn't understand words like *eschatology* or *soteriology,* but they could understand stories about farmers and disobedient sons. And he could have said things like "love your neighbor" until he was blue in the face, but telling the Good Samaritan story (Luke 10) does the job so much better. And regarding more spiritual things, the prophets talk about Israel straying and God's willingness to accept them back, but nothing gets the picture across any better than the Prodigal Son (Luke 15). It's all about boiling complicated teaching down so that ordinary folks can understand—*The Complete Idiot's Guide to God.*

Much about this theory rings true. Jesus certainly did want to reach the ordinary folks rather than just the religious elite. You can hear him throughout the gospels explaining and defending this controversial practice: It is not the healthy who need a doctor, but the sick. The damage to his reputation was so serious that the religious elite called him "a friend of tax-collectors and sinners," which is tantamount to calling him a "known associate of politicians and gangsters."

I believe that Jesus was seeking to reach the ordinary people, but what I object to is saying that he used parables to make the teaching easy to understand. It's a nice enough thought, but it doesn't fit with what's presented in the gospel, nor with the roundabout character of the parables.

The really difficult bit comes early: Mark 4.

Ten verses into that chapter, Jesus has been telling one of his best-known stories, the Parable of the Sower. You remember the one. Some seeds fell here and got choked by weeds, some there and wilted in the sun, some got picked off by birds, but a few fell on good ground and bore fruit— a hundred kernels harvested for every one planted.

It's actually a story that Jesus might have told to that guy in the leather jacket (who objected that Jesus was not the greatest teacher). It is probably intended to explain why, although he taught crowds, so few followed, and why that didn't trouble him. He was "broad casting" the seeds every-where and those who had ears would hear.

Now according to the Mrs. Bayster School of Parable Interpretation, the listeners should come backstage and tell Jesus how great it was to finally understand such compli-cated stuff. Instead we find the disciples coming to Jesus and saying, "That was great. But what in the world was it about? We just don't get it." This is, of course, fairly typical of the disciples, especially in Mark's gospel, where they misunderstand nearly everything. It's as if their idea of following Jesus was scurrying along beside him looking the wrong way—so much so that they would smack into lamp-posts and slide slowly to the ground with Xs for eyes and cartoon birds tweeting in circles round their heads.

If Jesus' use of parables really was an attempt to sim-plify things enough for simple people to understand, the attempt failed with the disciples. They still didn't get it and told him so.

Otherwise...

We still might think that Jesus intended to dumb down his teaching, but the disciples were just *so* thick that absolutely nothing could penetrate their lamppost-hardened skulls. But then there's the extraordinarily troublesome verses 10 to 12 of Mark 4. Before explaining the Parable of the Sower in some detail, Jesus begins by telling the disciples why he speaks in parables in the first place. He certainly seems to be saying that he doesn't want everyone to understand.

"To you," he says, "has been given the secret of the kingdom of God, but to those on the outside everything is given in parables in order that they might see it without getting it and hear it without understanding it. Otherwise they might turn and be forgiven."

The physicist Niels Bohr once said about quantum mechanics that anyone who isn't deeply shocked by the implications of the theory hasn't understood it. So with this statement of Jesus. Any pupil of Mrs. Bayster's who has read my paraphrase and not been shocked hasn't really read it. Some have probably looked up Mark 4:10–12 by now, hoping I'm wrong. My translation sounds awful: "in order that they might see it without getting it . . . otherwise they might turn."

If by chance you *have* looked it up, you'll find it offensive. Only the paraphrases, like Eugene Peterson's *The Message,* manage to soften it. Could Jesus be saying that he tells parables precisely to keep any old hearer from understanding what he was saying? So only those to whom the mystery or secret is given are on the "inside"? How can this possibly be right?

Far from being stories that clarify, it looks as though his purpose was to hide the truth, to deliberately make it "misunderstandable." From what Jesus appears to be saying, these are more like codes or riddles to be solved than like plain teaching. Indeed the gospel of Mark sets up a contrast between parables and plain teaching, telling us that Jesus spoke in parables to the crowd, but when he was alone with the disciples he spoke plainly (Mark 4:34).

If you have looked these verses up to check me, you may find that the bulk of verse 12 is set off as poetry, or is at least in quotation marks. This is because Jesus is quoting from the prophet Isaiah. You might think this helps a little bit: the phrase "otherwise they might turn" isn't Jesus himself but Jesus quoting and warning people that they may be acting like those in Isaiah's time. Not that Jesus delights in incomprehensible code language; he may be resigned to it. Like the cup he has to drink, perhaps this is how it has to be.

But no, that doesn't completely solve our problem. Even if Jesus is quoting, he's the one who is teaching in parables. He *chose* to teach and explain himself this way.

Secret and Mystery

This, at last, brings us to the heart of not only Jesus' style of telling parables but also of our larger concern in this book, his habit of asking questions. When Jesus tells the disciples that the "secret of the Kingdom of God" has been given to them, the Greek word is not about secret knowledge, as the translations might lead you to believe. No, it's *musterion* or mystery. The distinction between a mystery and a secret is preserved in English usage as well as the

Greek, though we hardly ever think about it. With a secret, knowledge is being withheld—there are facts or concepts you're not given. A mystery is very different. The concepts and facts are not hidden; on the contrary, you are immersed in them and they are so thick around you that you can't see the woods for the olive trees.

The classic mystery novels are just like this. After the body is discovered and the detective is roused from his or her rented seaside cottage, fact after fact presents itself: that woman has a preference for that size shoe; that painter was found without any white in his palette; the diamond pendant fashioned in the shape of a London cab once belonged to the butler's great-grandmother. The challenge is not that information is secret—being withheld by the author—but rather the opposite: The revelations whistle by your head too fast for you to sort them out or see them in perspective. As with many riddles, you also often need some lateral thinking.

With a secret, you're on the outside; with a mystery, you're in the thick of it, like those sidekicks trailing around after the master detective. Even when they're told who did it, they still can't see the significance of the green thread found caught on the rough edge of the picture frame in the guest bedroom the night before the murder.

In most translations of Mark 4, therefore, there is a specific connection between verses 11 and 12. Some have gotten the secret, or better, the mystery. For everyone else, it's a parable—still only a riddle (verse 11). And, not surprisingly, given the nature of riddles, those are the people in danger of seeing but perceiving, hearing but not understanding (verse 12).

Now we're in a position to notice something else. Verse 11 does not specifically say "to those outside, *all my teaching* is in parables" but rather "*everything* is in parables." It's just possible he's saying that his teaching is no different than the rest of existence and creation. Everything around us, including his teaching, presents humanity with something akin to a riddle.

That's why Jesus' teaching isn't data-rich—if it were information that was being withheld in secret-like fashion, then we'd expect the teaching to be providing the missing bits. But if Jesus the teacher diagnosed a different deficiency, then it would be only natural for his teaching to be correspondingly different. And this, in turn, perhaps exonerates our dim-witted disciples a wee bit. It may not be about understanding after all, and their teacher may not have expected them to fully comprehend. Indeed it may not be understanding and enlightenment that *we're* supposed to be seeking and finding either.

It is simply amazing how many great people in the history of Christianity have missed the point of the parables by looking for information and, especially, theology. It seems only common sense to us nowadays that the parable of the Good Samaritan, which Jesus answered in response to the question "Who is my neighbor?" should be answering that question in some way. And virtually no one could talk about the parable nowadays without some attention being paid to the fact that Samaritans were generally hated by the Jews. But for centuries, the quest for information, for data about some religious secret, pretty much obliterated any such thrust in the answer. For guys like Origen and

Augustine, writing early in the history of the church—before people needed last names—the parable of the Good Samaritan was code. It was, for them, a beautiful allegory of the larger Christian story.

Here then is the secret code those early writers thought they'd broken. Does the story concern a man who was nearly dead and then helped? It *must* be a story about Christ helping the sinner. And so the man becomes symbolic of Adam. His wounds became his sins. The robbers were Satan and his minions. The priest and Levite who passed by were the Law and the Prophets. The Samaritan was, of course, Jesus himself. He bandages the guy's wounds (restrains our sins), brought him to an inn (the church), and spoke to the innkeeper (the apostle Paul? the angels in charge of the church? the Pope?) giving him two denarii (the two commandments of love God above all and your neighbor as yourself) and—nudge, nudge—told the innkeeper that he'd be coming back soon.

You've got to give them credit; that is one spiffy job of decoding. And I haven't even given you all of the details! But, um, just how would all of this answer the question that the man in the gospel story asked Jesus? Doesn't it leave to one side the most unusual choice in the parable of the hero being a Samaritan rather than a peasant-class Galilean? And why would Jesus have capped such an allegory with the words "Go and do likewise"?

We will look a lot more closely at what this parable really means in chapter 4. For the time being, though, it seems pretty clear that Jesus was not giving a cryptogram to decode as much as a story to be taken to heart—a mystery or riddle to ponder.

The Wedge

More than they are meant to inform, Jesus' riddles or parables, like much of his teaching, seem to be poking at you, forcing you to take one side or another. I think of them as a wedge. The hearers stand poised in an in-between place, and Jesus' teaching comes at them sharp side first, forcing them to lean one way or another, perhaps just the smallest of inclinations, but the widening bit of the wedge forces the issue further and further open. One of the best examples of how a parable can be used in this way comes in the Old Testament (2 Samuel 12), a famous interchange between the prophet Nathan and King David.

Even though God chose him and he wrote lots of pretty psalms and so on, David sometimes made some pretty bad mistakes. The one that concerns us here is the unfortunate business of Uriah and Bathsheba. You may remember the story: His royal highness saw this babe sunbathing on a roof and determined to have her for his own even once he'd found out that she was already happily married to one of David's most loyal colleagues. So he took her and eventually arranged to have her husband killed in such a way that the blame would not fall on him.

But you're never completely safe in a country where prophets cruise around with the right to free speech. Nathan found out about it all. Now you or I in Nathan's shoes would probably have approached the problem differently. If we'd dared to do anything at all, we'd probably have protested and backed some alternative political party's candidate. Except, of course, that there weren't many alternative political parties to back at that point; at least not without us advocating and supporting a violent coup. Prophet Nathan was willing to confront the religious David face-to-face. I know that even if I had the guts for such a meeting, I would have acted very differently than Nathan did. "Right," I'd have said to myself. "Supreme and chosen monarch of Israel or not, it's time to call a duck-billed axe a duck-billed axe." I'm sure I would have brought along a good leather-bound Bible (although finding one in those days might have taken some doing). "Think about what you've done," I'd have thumped. "And read this!" And I'd fold my arms defiantly and tap my foot waiting for it to sink in that in the eyes of the Lord whom the king claimed to serve, David had been a Very Naughty Boy.

But Nathan doesn't play it the way that we would. Instead, the prophet acts as if he's complaining about something else entirely. There is a poor man, he says, who owns only one lamb which he loves. We're talking cute here. He ties a ribbon in the wool on its head and sets the table for it at meal times, and it looks at him like it understands when he talks to it. When the rich man who lives nearby has unexpected and hungry guests one day, the rich man decides to make the curry not from one of his own flocks but instead dices up Little Snookums.

"Off with his head," interrupts David, who is a sucker for stories like this. Then and only then does Nathan resolve the mystery of the story: "That man is you."

You see what's happened. David has been rendered defenseless by his own decree. Left to contemplate our own deeds, all of us are fence-sitters. We know too well all the circumstances and reasons and rationalisms. But we're able to make decisions about the story world; it's almost impossible not to interrupt the storyteller to give our opinion. (Might Nathan have begun with "I wanna ask ya somethin'"?) It's not simply that people need some "distance" to make the right choices, for the parable's success depends upon the hearer getting *inside* it. It is rather that we enter a situation afresh with new, more balanced perspective.

And the effect on the fence-sitter is like that of a pointed stick. You've got to move one way or the other. You've got to answer the question posed by the riddle. You cannot stay in the middle. It's like that wedge, taking the slimmest of openings, the slightest of leanings one way or the other, and forcing that "beginning of an inclination" to widen and become more and more itself.

This business of God reinforcing human choices is an idea firmly rooted in the Old Testament. In the story of the Exodus, the Bible talks about Pharaoh's heart hardening against the Israelites. Sometimes the text says that Pharaoh hardened his heart, other times that God hardened Pharaoh's heart. It seems unjust of God to punish Pharaoh when God was the one egging on Pharaoh's opposition to the Israelites, until you realize that it was Pharaoh's decision that God confirmed and strengthened.

And that's one of the classic pictures of free will: the interpretation of that famous Holman Hunt painting of Jesus standing at the door. The Scripture from which it is derived may mean something slightly different, but the image is correct nevertheless. Jesus stands at the door and knocks, but he will only confirm our decision. Like the widow in one of his own parables, he is persistent and after a while we cannot ignore him. We will either shout, "Oh, all right, already. Come on in," or, "Will you just go away and leave me alone." And it is that choice that he confirms in us.

Not even Christians truly feel comfortable with the idea that "just because someone doesn't believe in Jesus, God will consign them to hell for eternity." That phrasing of the matter makes it seem arbitrary and capricious. It is more understandable, as well as accurate, to say that when someone tells the Lord to just go away and leave them alone, he does go away. And leaves them. Alone.

Like Nathan's story for David, Jesus' parables and questions and perhaps everything that he did were intended to make fence-sitting less comfortable, to cause us to make a choice. That must be the meaning of the difficult passage in Mark 4 about understanding parables. He speaks the way that he does because he wants people to resolve themselves into those who have ears to hear and those who do not. Any god who is worthy of the title could force allegiance, but any god worthy of the title will not do so. But don't be surprised if he does force clarity about that allegiance.

The parables, even the short one-sentence ones we looked at toward the beginning of the chapter, are meant to provoke a response. In that way, even when they don't end in question marks, they're very like questions. As it happens, Jesus asked questions even more often than he told parables or riddles. And he probably used them to accomplish similar goals. In the next chapter, we'll look at some of the questions he asked within parables—questions you think you could answer with your eyes shut, but which instead force your eyes to open wide.

Questions for Reflection and Discussion

1. It's not just Jesus; Nathan is just one of the Old Testament figures who used parables, and it appears that many of the rabbis of Jesus' day also did. Are there situations in which it would be appropriate for people today to use parables?

2. From the evidence that we have in the book of Acts and the epistles, the use of parables (either their own or Jesus') in the early church is remarkably scarce. Why might that be?

3. Choose a favorite parable, find it in one of the gospels—at whom did Jesus aim it? What sort of decision might it have been provoking them to make?

4. I've suggested that "understanding" might not have been the most important thing Jesus expected from his followers. Is it really possible or fair to commit yourself to someone or something that you don't fully understand?

Chapter Two

Questions Easily Answered

Which of the two did what his father wanted?
Which will be more grateful?

That's Correct

On some occasions, Jesus asked questions that had a single, particular, sometimes self-evident answer. In a few striking cases, these questions have a close connection with a type of rebuking we'll look at more closely in chapter 5. Examples are when Jesus hammered his disciples with a series of questions, including some with obvious answers: "When I fed the five thousand, how much was left over?" to which the disciples reply feebly with the only answer possible: Twelve. "When I fed the four thousand, how much was left?" The answer had to be seven. If they'd answered, "Duh, three?" it would have been incorrect.

Some questions addressed to the Jewish leaders also seem to fit this pattern. Jesus sometimes asks them the obvious and does so as a rebuke or even attack. Faced with a facetious oral examination by some Sadducees, Jesus replies with a scornful reproach, "Have you not read in the book of Moses?" and recites the Torah to these ultra-orthodox Jews (Mark 12:18ff). Confronted with a challenge to the disciples' practice of picking and eating grain on the Sabbath, Jesus returns the challenge, "Have you never read what David did when he and his companions were hungry?" (Luke 6:3). On another Sabbath: "Which is lawful on the Sabbath: to do good or to do evil, to save life or to kill?" (Mark 3:4). The attack becomes even more fierce and personal when Jesus answers the question put to him, "Why do your disciples break the tradition?" with a question of his own, "And why do you break the command of God for the sake of your traditions?" (Matt. 15:2–3).

But not all of Jesus' questions are as charged with so much symbolism and significance to warrant a book about them. In the introduction, I've alluded to statistics about the large number of questions Jesus asks in the gospels. But some of them are quite innocent and ordinary. So, in a story about a healing, Jesus asked, "How long has he been like this?" Before doing his bread-and-fishes thing he asked the disciples, "How many loaves do you have?" Confronted with a man possessed by demons, he asked, "What is your name?" On meeting two disciples in heated discussion as they walked, he asked, "What were you arguing about on the road?" In all of these cases, the questions are in the gospels because they and their answers are significant to the story, but these are questions used in a primarily innocent and pedestrian way. Jesus was a human being, whatever else he was, going about ordinary business as well as this divine mission.

Absurdities

Although some of the questions are innocent, Jesus also uses a very different type of question to force the crowds and the disciples to reevaluate their positions. He seems to delight in using these questions to conjure up absurd situations: "If the salt loses its saltiness, how can it be made salty again?" (Matt. 5:13). Well, it can't. This apparently silly little sentence shakes up the religious people of our day as well as Jesus' contemporaries. If your whole identity is tied up in being the salt of the earth, and you're found not to be salty, it's a pretty fundamental problem.

While lighting a candle for my children the other day, several things struck me about another of Jesus' seemingly absurd questions. "Do you bring in a lamp to put it under a bowl or under the bed? Instead, don't you put it on a stand?" (Mark 4:21). How fragile my match-flame was! When lighting the candle, I had to shield the flickering little flame of the match, covering it with my hand, rather than a bowl, against the breeze that could easily put it out. The candle's flame was stronger, though, and an oil lamp would be stronger still. The idea is of going to the trouble of lighting a lamp and then placing it somewhere that its light won't be visible. Hiding the lamp may prevent it from being extinguished, but it also defeats its whole purpose.

Probably everyone's favorite image from Jesus' absurd questions is the question he asked to point out the nature of hypocrisy and faultfinding. It's the image of people going around trying to remove specks of dust from other people's eyes, while all the time putting the stock of the local lumberyard to shame. "Why do you look at the speck of sawdust in someone else's eye and pay no attention to the plank in your own eye?" (Luke 6:41). This always seemed a slapstick image more suitable for the Three Stooges than Jesus. I can see Timber-brain, with the long tree trunk protruding several feet from the front and the back of his head. He turns toward Speck-eye, "Here, I'll fix that eye of yours in no time." But when he turns his head, it causes the whole tree to sweep in a huge arc. Behind him a well-dressed portly couple are completely bowled over, tea cups and saucers flying, while in front of him, Speck-eye is also whacked off his feet. "Wait. Where'd everybody go?"

In all these cases, the images and questions are acting as parables. Jesus teaches by asking questions to which you already know the answers. But while the answers may be self-evident, the implications are wide and require much thought. He leaves you to begin to make the connections. There is a pattern here that we'll see again and again in Jesus' questions. The whole story starts with the situation, perhaps even a question from someone else to Jesus. Jesus then responds with a story or image which leads directly to (or even incorporates) one of his questions. That question or the answer to it has a direct effect on the original questioners in their situations, but also can have an effect on the readers of the story these thousands of years later.

One of Jesus' most famous stories is that of a prodigal son, his father, and his older brother (Luke 15:11–32). But he also told a shorter and less well-known story about a father with two sons (Matt. 21:28–31). In this one, both sons stay at home, though one of them stays put more than the other.

This story begins with a question: "What do you think?" It's Richie again, isn't it? I wanna ask ya somethin'. But Jesus does get around to actually asking a question, as you'll see.

In the parable, the father asks the first son to go and work in the vineyard. The text never actually uses the word *adolescent,* but, like me, you may find it hard to picture the son any other way but wearing jeans and slouching. He unplugs one earphone from his walkman to reply snottily, "No, I will not." Such a bald refusal of respect is totally unlike Middle Eastern culture and would have shocked the original hearers. It is as if he had shouted an obscenity to the father. One simply does not say "no" to one's father. The chief priests and elders will not often have encountered such disrespect and disobedience. Hearing the story thus far, they would think that that boy should be taught a lesson. Jesus has set them up magnificently for the coming surprise.

Before that, though, the second son displays a more common kind of disobedience. Given the same command, the second son not only responds in the affirmative but uses a respectful title. "I will, sir," he assures his dad. I bet his hair is combed and his t-shirt is ironed as well. But whether he really intends to do as he's told or not, somehow he never gets around to it. In the end, he has not only disobeyed but lied.

This is a kind of disobedience the Jewish leaders would have encountered much more frequently than the rude first son.

In the meantime the first son has had a change of heart. And this is not unrealistic in domestic situations featuring such blatant rudeness. It's one of the reasons having it out is better than bottling it all up. Once you voice your feelings, you begin to hear them objectively and realize how selfish they are. Despite (or perhaps because of) his harsh words, he works in the vineyard after all.

Now here's the best bit: Jesus follows the story with one of those obvious questions. "Which of the two did what his father wanted?" Those representatives of the religious establishment had no choice but to affirm that the son who had been scandalously disrespectful was, at the end, a more dutiful son. That son was better than the one who said the right words, who caused no scene, who was, in fact and not coincidentally, more like the chief priests and elders themselves and less like the "sinners" with whom Jesus spent so much of his time. It reminds me of some tennis matches I've seen. One second, we're all balanced on the end of our seats in the tension of the tie-break. The next, a well-placed serve zings by at 110 mph and it's over. Jesus leads, one set to love. New balls, please.

Two Debtors

Jesus also gave a few multiple-choice questions about debtors. The first is a story Jesus told about an unmerciful servant (Matt. 18:23–35). Peter has asked his master how many times he should forgive someone. Jesus replies with a story, using numbers that he has inflated to comic proportions. Some scholars reckon a "talent" was the equivalent of about fifteen years of wages. In Jesus' story, the servant owed his master ten thousand of those talents! What had this servant done with that much money? How could anyone borrow that much and still be working as a servant? We're talking about enough cash to buy your own multibedroom ziggurat on the banks of the Euphrates, a stretch-sedan chair with leather interiors, and enough left over for a lifetime supply of pomegranates, peeled grapes, and a matching pair of fan-waving servants of your own.

Of this debt the king forgives his servant.

It turns out that the servant himself has also lent out some of this king's ransom, and his buddy owes him a much smaller but still considerable amount—about half a year's wages. The king in the story asked, "Shouldn't you have had mercy on your fellow-servant just as I had on you?" That's precisely the question Jesus is asking Peter as well. If God has forgiven the huge debt you owe him, you've got a lot of forgiving of your own to do before you begin to catch up.

The chain reaction that we see here is typical of Jesus. He starts with a life situation such as Peter forgiving someone. From this he constructs a story. The story concludes with a question about the story. But though the question applies directly to the characters and actions within the story-world, it becomes a question aimed at the hearer. We're back to the life situation from which we began. And this last question becomes a question that challenges the reader of the story as well.

The Money-Lender

The next story comes in a very tense situation. It is some-what different and the underlying situation is similar to the stories of the two sons. Jesus was a dinner guest at the house of a Pharisee named Simon. Although this guy has invited Jesus to a meal, he has neglected some of the most basic elements of hospitality in that culture: He didn't greet him, he didn't provide water for him to wash up from his travels, and so on. Evidently, Simon doesn't intend to honor Jesus, or else he would have shown him some of the then-common courtesies. Rather, the situation reminds me of some TV or radio talk-show interviewers. The only inten-tion in talking to "the guest" is to ridicule, embarrass, or trivialize them. So Simon is probably thinking along these lines: If the crowds are making a fuss about this Jesus of Nazareth, very well. Jesus of Nazareth will then be invited to make an appearance—but at Simon's house and on Simon's terms. And Simon will make sure that everyone sees that he is not overly impressed, and that he is in a position to give or withhold favors. At least that's how the Pharisee planned it. But there were two things he hadn't anticipated.

The first was the unscheduled visit of the woman who "had led a sinful life." Simon's dinner party was not held inside behind locked doors, but outside where even the unin-vited could notice how important Simon was. But this also left the party open to a bit of gate-crashing. The woman washed and anointed Jesus' feet, and Simon knew who and what she was. Can you imagine the expression on his face as he looked at her and then at Jesus, the so-called holy man who allowed this sinful woman to touch him? Simon didn't reckon on her being there, but she only confirmed the bad things he'd heard about Jesus. The polite thing, of course, is not to say a thing about it—much the same as when someone today inadvertently makes a rude noise at a fancy dinner party.

The second thing he hadn't planned on was Jesus' willingness to be blunt. In that society, as in many cultures today, politeness dictates that guests must praise their hosts. Whatever the host does and whatever the host serves is, you must pretend, the most wonderful thing in the world—you cannot believe and do not deserve such luxury. Thank you, thank you, thank you soooo much. Simon did not reckon with Jesus' capacity for rebelling against mere social conventions. He starts with a laser-guided stealth story.

"Simon, I have something to tell you" is how the attack starts. This is an odd reversal of Richie's ploy. Here Jesus offers to *tell* Simon something, when he actually has a *question* in mind all along: "A man forgives two of his debtors. The first owed five hundred, the second owed just fifty. Which of the two debtors will be more grateful to the merciful money-lender?"

As with the two sons question, only one answer fits, and Simon perhaps laughingly gave it, still unaware of where this was all leading. "I suppose the one who had the bigger debt cancelled." That's when the situation explodes and spins out of control, as Jesus violates politeness and social norms, managing to be rude in three ways. First, in front of all the guests, he recounts Simon's failings as a host: there was no water for footwashing and so on. Second, Jesus openly refers to the woman, rather than politely ignoring her. "Do you see this woman?" he asks Simon. This forces him to acknowledge her presence, as well. Mentioning her is uncouth enough, but Jesus goes further and compares a woman who has led a sinful life favorably to Simon the devout Pharisee. She has supplied what was lacking in the hostly duties and honors which he had left undone. Is he suggesting that Simon should be in some way in her debt? Finally and possibly worst of all, he then addresses her— again publicly and directly. A man speaking to an uninvited woman of bad reputation. Scandalous!

Implications of the Obvious Answers

Jesus used questions with obvious answers to bring his message home. This happens again and again in the gospels. In story after story he used the obvious question to stop people in their tracks and make them think again about the implications. Once he asked, "Who touched me?" It sounds like one of those innocent questions such as "How long has he been like this?" and "What is your name?" But when Jesus asked, "Who touched me?" he was in the middle of a crowd (Luke 8:45)! You're packed into the commuter train, executives' faces smushed against the glass in the doors, and someone asks, "Excuse me, did you touch my clothes?" A woman had touched the hem of his garment in order to be healed and then tried to sneak away. She probably imagined that she could go unnoticed and unremarked. "Who touched me?" is not just an ordinary question. He asks so that she'll answer. And he wants her to answer because she must learn to "own" her actions. Furthermore, she must realize that Jesus knows and approves. And still further, she needs to learn that it is her faith that has saved her rather than some automatic magical power (8:48).

Similar and yet very different is the woman in Mark 7:24–30. She sought deliverance for her daughter and was not shy in approaching Jesus and asking for it, despite being a Gentile rather than a Jew. He recognized her faith too, but encouraged it in a bizarre way. In reply to her request for help, Jesus confronted her with a challenge very like a question: "It can't be right to take the children's bread and feed it to the dogs." Talk about obvious answers. No, it cannot be right to feed dogs from the children's plates. But she will not give the standard reply and does not apologize. Instead, she will ad-lib. The obvious answer is not always the one that Jesus wanted. But more about *her* in chapter 7.

Next we'll look at a very different use of questions. Jesus sometimes seems to avoid issues and other people's inquiries by using questions as an evasive maneuver: He ducks their questions with questions of his own.

Questions for Reflection and Discussion

1. There's a well-known teaching technique known as the "Socratic Method." When a student claims ignorance of a complex idea, the teacher asks questions about bits of the idea—questions that both teacher and student do know the answer to. By the end of the process, students not only come away with the complex idea, but the realization that they knew it all along. How is this method like and unlike what Jesus does with these easily answered questions?

2. As with the parable of the two sons, some of the parables and questions fit as easily into our culture as they did into first-century Palestine. The details of some others, like the servant who owed money to the king or even the prodigal son, place them firmly in an ancient setting. If Jesus were making those points today, how would he reset those parables?

3. The story about Jesus asking the woman, "Who touched me?" in Luke 8:45 is full of peculiarities. Does Jesus' power flow out of him in a way that he can detect energy spikes and dips? Is touching the hem of his garment really enough, or does he consciously heal people? What does he accomplish by asking, "Who touched me?" when the woman had already been healed?

4. In our own day, the ultrasuccessful CEO of Pepsi, John Sculley, left a lucrative and safe job to take a job in the computer industry—all because of a question. Apple chief Steve Jobs asked him, "Do you want to spend your life selling sugary water or do you want to come with me and change the world?" Have you ever asked or been asked a deceptively simple question that changed the course of someone's life?

Chapter Three

Ducking Questions with Questions

By whose authority . . . ?
Whose picture is on the coin . . . ?

Questions and Recipes

Have you ever played the game where two people have to carry on a conversation, but they are only allowed to speak in questions? It becomes fairly contrived after a while, doesn't it? Don't you find that you pretty quickly degenerate into just prefacing statements with phrases like "Isn't it true that. . ." or "Don't you find. . ."? How many questions in a row have I managed in this paragraph? Can you imagine what an Olympic-level player of this game would be like?

Jesus certainly would have made the Israeli team. One of his most striking characteristics is the way that he handled difficult questions hurled at him high speed. He not only neutralized them, but somehow managed to send new questions hurtling back at his adversaries. Then he'd watch his conversational opponents tie themselves up in knots deciding which way to reply.

A good example of this kind of behavior is found in the acrimonious slanging match between Jesus and the so-called authorities recorded in Luke 20:1−8 (though parallels are found in Matthew and Mark as well). There's bad news cooking from the very first verse. Luke could almost have written it up as a recipe card. Sometimes you can tell within a few ingredients whether this is the kind of recipe you can handle or not.

This one sounds like I could tackle it:

> 4 chicken breasts
> salt and freshly ground black pepper
> 2 pints chicken stock
> 1 T. fresh ginger, sliced
> 1 clove garlic, sliced

This one, on the other hand, sounds like I'm likely to drop my apron and run:

> 1 duck gizzard
> 4 dried Chinese mushrooms, soaked for 20 minutes, drained, stemmed, and diced
> 15 g. dried shrimp
> 8 dried chestnuts, soaked overnight, simmered until soft and chopped
> 2 T. Chinese wine

In Luke 20:1, it's not so much the ingredients themselves as much as the combination and the order in which he stirs them into the pot. There's Jesus, teaching; the people, listening; the chief priests; the teachers of the law; the elders. We're not preparing Boneless Duck with Eight Precious Stuffings here . . . we're cooking up some high explosives.

A Question of Authority

In front of an interested public, the chief priests, the teachers of the law, and the elders, full of hatred for Jesus (see two verses earlier, Luke 19:47), hit him with the confrontational question: "Who gave you the authority to do these things?" Yet, like those made-up questions "computer experts" insert in their columns in order to give some tip they've discovered, the question Jesus faces has the hallmarks of a perfect set-up or "straight line" for the hero of Christianity. Politicians would do it this way:

"I'll go over to the crowd and start teaching, then you pretend to interrupt and ask me, 'Who gave you this authority you've got?' and then I'll answer, 'God himself has given me this message for you,' then you look surprised."

But the story does not proceed that way at all. Perhaps "Who gave you this authority?" is a misinterpretation of what was being asked. It takes a little thought to appreciate the social dynamics of the situation. Jesus' questioner is not one of his own social class asking what makes *him* special. Rather, it is a crowd of his "superiors." You have to read a patronizing tone into what they ask him: "Pardon us, but who exactly gave you permission to do these things?"

If you want to exasperate a rebel, there are a few questions almost guaranteed to do the trick. They tend to begin with phrases like "Who gave you permission to . . . ?" or "Who said you could . . . ?" What irritates is the implication underneath the question. By the very nature of the question, the person being challenged in this way is assumed not to have sufficient authority in themselves. And, even more infuriating, any reply to the question loses. Who gave you permission? It cannot have been those of responsibility in the Temple, the chief priests, because they're there. It cannot have been those whose sphere of responsibility was the Law, for the teachers of the Law were there. Nor can it have been the social leaders, for the elders were also there. There's only one reply left, it seems. And "No one gave me permission" sounds like a defeat.

When I was growing up, the only winning reply to "Who said you could do that?" was the stunning rejoinder "It's a free country." But Jesus is not living in a free country; his is occupied. Jesus could easily and truly have replied, "There is no Roman law against it," or, "Jewish tradition gives anyone the right to do as I am doing." But either of these replies would be implicitly accepting the power of Roman law or Jewish tradition as an authority confining him.

The typical Christian would want Jesus to say, "By God the Father's authority and not merely with his permission, in fact, but by God's instruction." But that's very hard to pull off in this situation. The chief priests, the teachers of the law, and the elders would not have reckoned it a possibility. Almost everyone thought *them* to be the interpreters of God's authority on earth in a much more concrete way than the clergy are thought to be today. Imagine confronting the employees of a branch office of your bank. Can you really envisage winning an argument in which you claim that *you* know better than *they* what the bank wants from you in the way of a withdrawal form? "Who said you could use *that?!*" That's our situation here. There *will* come a time for Jesus to treat this as a straight line, to engage in such a straight-speaking showdown, but this isn't it.

Fancy Footwork

So how does Jesus reply to this serve to the body? I'm still not sure whether it's a crosscourt volley or a lob, but the first key is his footwork. Look at him dance: Verse 2: "Who gave you this authority?" Verse 3: He replied, "I wanna ask ya somethin'." "Tell me, John's baptism—was it from heaven or of human origin?" A question for a question.

This return question is aimed directly at a weakness in the Establishment. Their handling of John the Baptist was far from exemplary. Such an arbitrary execution caused by the ruler's overreaction to the dancing of a young girl must have been deeply embarrassing to the religious elite. They didn't like the way John rejected the priestly calling he might have followed as his father's eldest son, nor did they like the things he was saying. They were probably jealous of the crowds that he attracted. They rationalized their opposition by noting that it was likely to attract attention and retribution from Rome by appearing to be a popular uprising. The Jewish leaders might have thought, *What did he expect?* but they will have been even more repelled by Herod's actions than by John's. Herod's was the worse of the two "evils" or unpleasantnesses. But they would much prefer, religiously and politically, to remain neutral.

The word *neutral* and the name *Jesus* can only rarely be used comfortably in the same sentence. When the so-called authorities try to put Jesus on the spot, he manages to turn the huge machine round so the light, heat, and pressure falls on them instead. "Tell me, John's baptism . . . was it divine or human?"

There are many things about the Bible I don't understand, but one of the greatest mysteries, at least to me, is why guys like these never say, "We asked you first!" while they have the chance. That's what Richie or I would have done. But no, they feel the spotlight on them once again, and they scramble for a way to reply.

It is satisfying to see these big shots caught in a dilemma just as ticklish as the one in which they'd attempted to place Jesus. But it is a qualitatively different question. Theirs to him was apparently open-ended but in practice rhetorical. "Who said you could do this?" From the question alone, it looks as though any answer was possible, but the only answer that they expected was, "Nobody gave me permission." Jesus' question, on the other hand, has the two possible answers clearly delimited within it. John's authority was either of human origin or it was from God.

Whoa! This is not the kind of distinction that these Jewish authorities would have made. By their way of thinking, the distinction is not human authority or divine authority. To their way of thinking, you have either gone through the "proper" channels of authority (namely themselves) or you haven't. In setting up the human/divine distinction in the evaluation of John, Jesus is subtly leading the listeners (if not the authorities) to change their categories. The question forces them to think of Jesus' own authority on human/divine terms. It also, more damagingly, relocates the authority of his would-be inquisitors into those categories. His next question could easily be, "And *your* authority, chief priests, lawyers, elders . . . ?"

But they don't have time to worry about that in the heat of the moment; they've got the J. the B. question to answer. They remind me of chess endgames I've played and lost. The opposition's hand is in front of their face, sighting down their index fingers as it twitches back and forth, working through possible moves on the board: "If I go here, he'll go there then I'll be sunk; but if I go there, he'll take that and I'll be sunk." But they are not thinking about the question itself, not debating whether John was God's messenger or not; they are focusing on a marketing and political spin. It looks for all the world as though they would be willing to give *either* answer. They will choose their answer not on the basis of whether it is true or not, but on the basis of the reaction their answer will receive by the crowd and what position the answer will place them in.

You have to love it: The Pharisees find themselves in almost exactly the dilemma in which they hoped to pin Jesus. There simply is no good answer. They have to try and bow out of the contest with the feeble, "It's not possible to say with any certainty." And Jesus treats *that* response with the scorn it deserves. And he takes it as sufficient ground, furthermore, to decline to answer their original question.

He has, in fact, ducked their question by asking one of his own. It isn't, in all likelihood, that he's not considered the matter—that he has no answer to their question in his own mind. Nor is it likely to be because he's afraid of giving an answer, as they were. We'll come back to the motive behind his refusal to answer later in the book.

Had they been a little bit quicker, they might have bounced another question back at Jesus just as he'd bounced back with his:

"Who said you could do these things?"

"I'll ask you a question, who said J. the B. could do the things *he* did?"

"Oh, yeah, well we'll see you and raise you one. On whose authority is *Caesar* acting?"

As it happens, Jesus' immediate opponents don't think of this quickly enough. But someone does think of it, and soon. For in all of the gospels that contain this story of Jesus' authority questioned, there follows, after only a story or two, the more famous passage in which Jesus is asked whether a Jew should pay taxes to pagan Rome or not.

Heads I Win, Tails You Lose

I remember a cartoon from the *New Yorker* magazine that featured a busy but contented-looking Satan. He was sitting behind a wooden desk, incongruously situated in the middle of one of the caverns of Hell, doing his paperwork. On his desk were two trays, moderately full of sheaves of paper. Instead of being labeled "in" and "out," the trays read "damned if you do" and "damned if you don't."

At the outset of the story about taxes to Caesar (Mark 12:13; Matt. 22:16), Jesus faced an unlikely pairing: the Pharisees and Herodians. Their different characteristics foreshadow the two sides of the dilemma in which they will try to trap Jesus: purity of moral and religious devotion (represented by the Pharisees) or acknowledgement of the real world of compromise with the Roman Empire (represented by the Herodians). Even if it's making too much of these verses to see any alliance formed, the fact of them working together at all is ironic. The Pharisees have tainted their purity by collaborating with the collaborators at least to the extent of setting up the Herodians to do their dirty work. The Herodians also demonstrate *their* tolerance by working alongside the Pharisees in this matter. The reader is probably meant to be aware of these tensions and ironies, although the characters in the story are not.

Jesus' opponents probably see him as a celebrated loud-mouth and an "armchair quarterback." "It's easy for *him*," they may well have thought, "wandering around with no real responsibilities and no one to answer to." They must have hoped their question would go some way toward landing him on the playing field with the pros. They hand him the ball and long for him to play badly and get trounced.

If the Satan cartoon describes the problem the authorities faced over deciding about John the Baptist's authority, it may also fairly describe Jesus' dilemma here. Rome is an occupying army, a pagan government usurping God's authority in the land he gave to his people. Is it right to pay tribute and show honor and submission to such a figure as the self-styled "divine" Emperor? Were Jesus to answer, "Yeah, okay. Pay the taxes," it might well be taken as a denial that Israel as a nation belonged to God and that they should serve him alone. If, on the other hand, he were to answer, "No; we owe allegiance to no one but the Lord God," he will be acting against Rome, virtually preaching noncompliance and rebellion, and would be liable to arrest and punishment. Again, although *we readers* know that Jesus is preparing to submit himself to arrest at the hands of Judaism and Rome, the characters in the story do not—they assume that such a fate would be the end of him.

It is a dilemma; either answer loses. But Jesus' opponents are probably in little doubt which way he will choose. The Pharisees clearly expect Jesus to side with them against the Roman Empire. This was the reason for having the Herodians along (as Luke spots with perfect vision, Luke 20:20). But it is also made clear from the way that they ask their question. They set him up with flattery—surely *he* will look beyond earthly authority: "We know that you are a man of integrity. You aren't swayed by [human beings], because you pay no attention to who they are; but you teach the way of God. . . . Is it right to pay . . . tax to Caesar or not?" (Mark 12:14). This question expects the answer to be "Never mind the claims of the human Caesar, give tribute to God and serve him alone."

They ask, "Should we pay or shouldn't we?" But their hypocrisy is shown by the way that they are not really interested in what they should do; they are not really interested in knowing what Jesus thinks—whether he sides with them or not. Their only interest is to get him to incriminate himself. Oddly, Jesus' use of questions may be exactly the opposite—he doesn't give a satanic in-tray about the ramifications, the *only* thing he cares about is whether you side with him or not.

It will not surprise you when I tell you that Jesus answered their question with some questions of his own.

His first was a quick throw-away, "Why are you trying to trap me?" and is a much more profound question than it seems at first glance. After all, the incriminating answer they're waiting for from Jesus is one that they themselves would want to give. Why try to trap someone who believes as you do? So Jesus points them to consider their motives. Why would they want to harm someone who agrees with them about the character of God and our duty to him? It cannot be for good motives. As with many of Jesus' apparent throw-away lines, if the conversation partners had considered the short comment, they could have corrected their attitude.

What Belongs to Whom?

But next comes the more famous question. Jesus often teaches with props, but he usually uses things and sights that he runs across; it's rare for him to request a visual aid as he does here with the denarius coin. And once the coin is produced, he works wonders with it.

He asks about portrait and inscription: "Whose image and words are stamped into it?" As with Nathan's parable to David and with parables generally, the audience finds themselves answering first and thinking about the implications next. There is no doubt in anyone's mind whose picture that is on the coin. It isn't some long dead U.S. president; it's most probably the current emperor. And in a world without TV news and without newspaper front pages, this is probably the main way that people on the outskirts of the Empire had any idea of what their emperor looked like.

Nor could you mistake the inscription on it. These coins were not inscribed with some vague platitude or slogan. On any of the candidate denari, the main inscription proclaimed the Emperor's name and title, something along the lines of "Tiberias Caesar, son of the divine Augustus." There can be no doubt about to whom these words referred. All present with Jesus on that day would be certain that they came from a human empire and not from the Kingdom of God.

So on the surface level, answering Jesus' question is simplicity itself. These are Caesar's image and inscription. What's more, however, a coin containing those words and a graven image is not the kind of artifact that a good Jew should want. I wonder if the person whose coin was being borrowed felt a little worried about where this was leading.

Beyond the content of the answer being obvious, the very grammar of the answer is dictated by the grammar of the question. It pretty much has to be possessive: Whose? X's. The implication is, then, also obvious: "If you say it is X's, then give it to X," or as the old Bibles have it, "Render unto Caesar those things which are Caesar's" (KJV).

That's game and second set to Jesus. But wait! He didn't stop there. Jesus went on to use this piece of the coin of the realm to teach some profound Jewish theology. He does not stop with the things that are Caesar's. He goes on to say also, " . . . and give to God the things that are God's."

But what things *are* God's? So far no one has talked about what things belong to him, only about what things belong to Caesar. But perhaps Jesus has shown us how to find out what is God's. Insofar as he has given a method for determining that the coin is Caesar's, he has implicitly given a method for determining what it is that is God's. It's not hard—all you have to do is look for something bearing God's image and inscription on it. And this would ring some bells for his Jewish audience. The very first chapters of their Scripture tell them that humanity was made in the image of God. Image of God—image of Caesar. In effect, Jesus is telling them that they can give the coins to Caesar, but they themselves belong to God.

Ducking the Question

Does all this mean you should pay taxes or not? It turns out that Jesus has provided a rationale for either solution to the dilemma! The one who does pay taxes can still practice Jewish devotion by not confusing what is owed to each authority. The one who refuses can find support in the expansion of Jesus' exhortation to "give God what he is due," if paying taxes is considered to compromise that higher duty. What's more, some writers have suggested that by his reply, Jesus has even justified the refusal of *any* allegiance to Caesar. The making of graven images is pretty severely dealt with in the Ten Commandments. Jesus drew attention to the image on the coin as well as the inscription, which is likely to have been blasphemous from a Jewish perspective. His hearers are not just to give back the coins for which he has asked but to avoid using coins or participating in The System at all.

Jesus' answer is simple: a place for everything and everything in its place. And yet it is an answer packed with subtlety and complexity. Little wonder that all the gospels tell us that Jesus' opponents were amazed and astonished.

It's like the sporting event where you watch the arrogant loudmouth on that other team gain possession of the ball, hoping for him to do badly, to be shown up as the braggart he is. Five minutes later, you're shaking your head and admitting that perhaps that multimillion contract he signed at the beginning of the season wasn't too far off after all. The Pharisees are in just that place. They don't like Jesus any better, perhaps, but they cannot help but admire his performance. "Give to Caesar what is Caesar's and give God what is God's." It's nothing short of brilliant. Inspired, even.

But does it answer the question or not? He has avoided the trap, but has he also avoided the question? Is Jesus giving usable advice or merely lobbing the decision back into someone else's court? Is he equivocating or cutting to the core of the matter? Does he, perhaps, cut to the center of divine concern *precisely by* bypassing the immediate but shallow concerns of the questioners? This seems to be the case with our next few passages, which we'll explore in the next chapter.

Questions for Reflection and Discussion

1. Asked about the source of his authority, Jesus winds up saying, "Neither will I tell you," and we are never told what Jesus' answer would have been. The New Testament writers, obviously, thought that Jesus was acting entirely on God's authority. But what about Jesus himself—did he think so? How would we know?

2. Most Westerners at least feel as though their governments are much more in line with Christianity than Caesar was in line with Judaism. Are there, however, ways in which you have to choose between your Caesar and God? Are there tendencies in your government's recent actions that lead you to imagine having to make a choice?

3. Further on this point, is there any logical and consistent way for Christians to decide when civil disobedience is appropriate and when it's not, or is it always decided on a case-by-case basis?

4. Jesus ducked questions with questions to bypass immediate but shallow concerns; is it appropriate for us to be doing this? How can you tell when a question can be ducked and when it must be faced?

Chapter Four

Questions That Cut to the Center

What did Moses command you?
Who was neighbor to the man?

Testing Jesus

Wanting to test Jesus, the Pharisees asked, "Is it lawful for a man to divorce his wife?" (Mark 10:2). In today's world divorce is increasingly common, almost unremarkable. But none of us likes to be put on the spot about it. Breaking relational commitments made is an evil that causes immense damage to everyone involved; yet in many cases, it's difficult to see how such a message helps those people whose lives have already been torn apart. We want to speak out prophetically against a society whose values seem to make divorce so acceptable (almost palatable) while avoiding speaking in a judgmental way against real and vulnerable people caught up by the painful and complex business.

A glimpse at the historical perspective adds a touch of danger. In the Palestine of Jesus' day, divorce was not only emotionally sensitive but also politically sensitive. It's hard for us in the twenty-first–century West to remember that in many cultures it simply isn't safe to have an opinion. The account of John the Baptist's arrest and imprisonment in Mark 6:16–19 reminds us that it isn't healthy to speak out against the marital arrangements of the ruling family. Criticize too loudly and you could wake up with your head on the business end of a platter.

Were the Pharisees deliberately tempting Jesus into giving a "sound bite" that would make him an enemy of the rulers? As we've seen, this was certainly the motivation behind another question: "Should a good Jew pay taxes to the pagan emperor?"

But it is probably not the case here. We often forget that the Pharisees were not uniformly against Jesus. On at least one occasion, Pharisees specifically took his side against Herod—warning him that the despot was out looking to kill him (Luke 13:31–33). When Jesus replied, "You tell that fox . . ." did they smile conspiratorially at each other? Not all Pharisees, it would appear, wanted to see Jesus trapped and Herod triumphant.

Also, both Jesus and the gospel writers seem to treat this as a serious question rather than as a mere trap. Generally when people dig deep pits for Jesus to fall into, it is the plotters who land in it over their heads, and the gospel writers are delighted to say so. That is not how our story is slanted.

Why then does Mark say that the Pharisees were "testing" Jesus by asking him this?

There were, within Pharisaism, two different schools of thought about the hot topic of divorce. The differences occur because of the vague wording of Deuteronomy 24:1–4. It speaks of the husband finding "something indecent" about the wife whom he will divorce. One branch of the Pharisees took a very strict line and interpreted Deuteronomy's "something indecent" to mean that a divorce should only be granted in a case of sexual unfaithfulness.

The more moderate wing of the Pharisees read this "something indecent" in a more open way. Their line also seemed reasonable; the passage seems to center around the husband's *displeasure* with the wife rather than about the wife's *sinfulness*. The Mosaic law certainly had heavier penalties than mere divorce for acts of sexual indiscretion. This passage therefore, they argued, must refer to something less than adultery which incurs a lesser penalty. So these Pharisees allowed a much larger range of acceptable reasons for divorce, including some that we would regard as trivial. It may be that the Pharisees in Mark 10 were "testing" Jesus in order to find out which of their groups he would side with: the strict or the loose.

Commandment or Concession?

The reply that comes is surprising, but typically Jesus. Whatever their reason for asking Jesus their question, he responds, not unusually, with a question of his own. "What did Moses command you?" he replied (Mark 10:3). It is interesting to note that this time his reason for replying with a question was not in order to duck theirs. He *is* willing to state his view and take a fairly firm line on it in the verses that follow. Why then does he ask them a question? In particular, why would he ask experts in the laws of Moses a question *about Moses?*

It cannot be that Jesus inquires because he is ignorant of what is written in the books of Moses and hoping to find out from the experts what is there. In fact, he went on to quote some of the passage that he apparently had in mind all along. It may have been that his reply, "What did Moses command you?" contained within it an implicit criticism. Here is the sting in Jesus' question: At first, it *looks* as though it revolves around the word *Moses*—"What did Moses say?" Indeed, the Pharisees' reply shows that they took the question this way. Moses did allow for divorce: Moses "permitted" this and that, came their reply.

This is precisely the sort of reply that allowed Jesus the tiger to pounce. Moses may have "permitted" such a thing, but that was *not* Jesus' question. He was not primarily asking about Moses, he was primarily asking about commands. Rather than paraphrasing the question, "What did The Lawgiver say about divorce?" Jesus' question should be paraphrased, "When do the Scriptures say you *must* divorce someone?" There is, of course, no *command* to divorce to be found in this controversial Old Testament passage! In fact, when we look seriously at Deuteronomy 24:1–4 we see that it was never intended to set out the conditions for divorce at all! It is rather to regulate remarriage in cases where there had been divorce. It does not say, "When one person does something indecent the spouse *must* divorce them." Nor does it even go so far as to say, "When one person does something indecent the spouse *should* divorce them." Rather it says, "If someone is in the position of having been divorced for this something indecent, here is how that position affects their future life."

Jesus pounces: Divorce, he says, comes about not because God's commands are firm, but because our hearts are hard. Moses' law permitted divorce. Now, he says, listen to what God intended. And then he quotes what he regards as the relevant passage, going further back in history and further into the intentions of the Creator God, quoting from the first chapters of Genesis rather than the middle of Deuteronomy. Divorce is a late concession rather than an intentional command.

What *Are* They Talking About?

Now of course many books have been written about Jesus' view of divorce. It's not an easy topic to resolve, and I won't even pretend to attempt to do so here. But have you noticed this: neither the Pharisees' question nor Jesus' question and reply are *about divorce* in the final analysis. The passage does go on to treat the question of divorce in its own right, but only after the Pharisees are away and Jesus is alone with his disciples.

The discussion with the Pharisees may have *featured* the topic of divorce. But what the discussion was truly *about* was the Pharisees' attitude toward the Scriptures and their attitude toward their own behavior. Jesus' question cuts to the center. His question exposes the Pharisaic debate on strict or loose interpretation for what it was then and what it is when we do it: A human attempt to justify ourselves.

Exploiting loopholes is not the same as living out the law. Exploiting loopholes can be using what the law does not say to subvert what the law intends. And Jesus pounced: "Look!" he said, "Look at what God *really* wanted."

Similarly, Jesus spoke of his followers putting their hand to the plough and not looking back. But often Christians today want to know, "Okay, we can't look back *per se* ... but what about peeking sideways?" How often are modern attempts at Bible study an attempt to define loopholes—to know how much we can get away with? This is precisely the attitude we see in the next story.

Perhaps we get to the heart of spiritual reality not by asking things, but by allowing ourselves to *be questioned*.

Not Quite the Story You Expected

Many people think they know the story of the Good Samaritan in Luke 10, but I would guess that not many people get the joke. We've seen that Jesus' parables often have stings in their tails, and this one is no exception. Again, someone approached Jesus to ask something, and again his reply, when it comes, is itself in the form of a question, or rather two questions this time: "What is written in the Law ... how do you read it?" and, later on, "Which of these was a neighbor to the man?"

In between these two questions Jesus tells his little story. The punch line, when he reaches it, will turn Jesus' questioner inside-out and upside-down. Jesus may as well have asked this "expert in the law," "And what does the world look like to you now?" All this from an innocent-sounding little tale about an unfortunate man and an unlikely rescue.

The key to getting the punch line is to put yourself in this expert's sandals. In reading the story of the Good Samaritan, how easily we overlook verses 25 and 29! It is an expert in the law who is questioning Jesus (v. 25), and he is asking his question in order to test Jesus and justify himself (vv. 25, 29). Now what did it mean to be an expert in the law? Sometimes we translate terms like this as "lawyer," but that may be a misleading term in our day. "Theologian" might be better. He was almost certainly a Pharisee, and like the Pharisees in the dispute about divorce, he was seeking to justify himself and his own view of the law. If the Pharisees in that other story were concerned to discover how much the law permitted a man in the matter of divorce, this man asked his question, "And who is my neighbor?" in a way that, in effect, could be translated, "How little can I do and still fulfill the law?" Some of us go through a similar exercise with our boxes of Christmas cards and address books on those years when we get around to Christmas cards at all. Where do I draw the line? Who is too close to be left out and who isn't? You say I must love my neighbor? Very well, but I want to know who it is that I must regard as a neighbor and who can be safely omitted.

A firm grasp on this background will allow us not only ears to hear the parable but also eyes to see Jesus' tongue in his cheek when he crafts his answer. Jesus is constantly suckering his audience into expecting one thing before giving them something else entirely. Consider the wording when the first passerby appears: Literally it starts out, "And *by chance* a priest...." Ah, this *is* a fortunate chance for the poor victim. God's servant will certainly undo the work of the evil men. But then help *does not* come through this high official.

But wait a second, it is a "priest" in the first instance. How is an "expert in the law," a theologian, likely to feel toward a priest? Just as "experts" were usually Pharisees, so also priests were almost certain to be Sadducees, concerned as they were with the affairs of the Temple. Although Pharisees and Sadducees were both Jews and could work together in such institutions as the High Council or Sanhedrin, they did not see eye to eye about a great many matters (see Acts 23 for the near riot that ensues when Paul mentions a bit of doctrine that the Pharisees like and the Sadducees do not). In our culture, members of political parties may furnish a good analogy. Sure, they sit in that big building together and act similarly, but they are certain to disagree about things. In particular, Sadducees and Pharisees disagreed pretty fundamentally on what religion is all about. For Sadducees, true religion has to do with Temple and sacrifice and rules that God set up in the first five books of the Scriptures. For the Pharisees, true religion had to do with the whole of the Old Testament Scripture and with making it relevant for their day. Pharisees wanted to teach the ordinary people to bring holiness into everything they did every day of the week, not only on the Sabbath or in the Temple.

So was there a smug smile on our Pharisee as he heard of the appalling lack of holy compassion in the life of this passerby priest? "How typical of a priest!" he will be saying

Jesus Asked

to himself. Similarly, the next person down the parable's road is no Pharisee or rabbi but another temple functionary, a Levite. A lesser figure than a priest, he will nonetheless have had important religious duties, responsibilities, and privileges in the Temple. And as with the figure of priest, our expert will not be too disappointed when the Levite also passes by without helping.

The stage is now set. Who will be the third person to pass down that road? Imagine yourself as the first hearer of the story. Imagine that instead of an ancient expert in the law, you are a member of one of our contemporary main political parties. The priest and Levite are well-placed members of the rival party. The story is clearly going somewhere; the third person is likely to be the one to save the day. Who would you expect to be this contrasting third person? Would you not be expecting the third person to be someone of your own political party? How very predictable, you'd be thinking. The third person will be just like me and he will help the unfortunate stranger, and Jesus will say, "That's who your neighbor is! Go and help unfortunate people because no one else will."

What Happened to Me?

But Jesus has a few more surprises up the sleeve of his robe. It isn't a member of your political party. It isn't a member of your rival political party. It isn't an independent candidate. It isn't even an ordinary citizen in "this great country of yours." It's some guy from whichever country you are currently sure is full of terrorists! In first-century terms, it's one of those despised Samaritans.

In some ways the modern organization "The Samaritans" makes a true understanding of this parable harder. In Jesus' day, his people would certainly not think about calling the Samaritans to talk to when life got a bit tough! In some ways, Samaritans were worse than foreigners to the Jews, because they were regarded as half-breeds. Samaritans were regarded as the descendents of the tribes of the northern kingdom of Israel who intermarried with non-Jews after the fall of the kingdom. For first-century Jews, it was like the difference between your enemies and those who are traitors. For Jesus to make such a person the "good" role model in the story went beyond surprising to being mildly offensive.

Now where are we? With whom is the reader or hearer meant to identify now? All story long the "expert in the law" will have been waiting for someone like himself to make an appearance and be a neighbor. Throughout the story he will have heard about people with whom he cannot identify: priests, Levites, and now a Samaritan. But wait, there *is* someone in the story in whom the hearer might see himself: the man who was beaten up by the robbers. We have not been told anything about that man's party alignments. Jesus' question at the end completes this flip of perspective. It is not "Who did the priest and Levite regard as neighbor, and who did the Samaritan regard as his neighbor?" Instead Jesus asks the question from the perspective of the victim, "Who did the victim regard as neighbor? Who became a neighbor to him?"

There is a clear relationship here with Jesus' teaching about the so-called Golden Rule: "Do to others as you would have them do to you." Do not ask, "Who *must* I see as a neighbor?" Ask instead, "Who would I want to see me as neighbor if I were in need?" Jesus has once again used his question and his parable to cut right through to the central matter. The problem isn't that of defining who is our neighbor, it is a problem of changing our attitudes from that of limiting our obligations to that of seeking to be of service. What he's asking for isn't accomplished as easily as expanding the Christmas card list to include terrorists. The problem isn't about the length of our list at all. It's about having a list mentality in the first place. It is a problem of changing our attitude—from that of seeking to limit our obligations to that of seeking to be available for service.

The man asked, "Who is my neighbor?" in order to find out who was not. Jesus wants us to ask, "Who *can be* my neighbor?"

Jesus tells this innocent-sounding story, with all its surprise twists and omissions, and then asks the "expert": "Which of these three do you think was a neighbor to the man who fell into the hands of robbers?" The expert, head spinning, could only gulp. No reply was possible except the one he gave, "The one who had mercy on him."

"In that case," Jesus might have said, "I think you have the answer to your question already.

"Any other questions?"

Questions That Cut

My advice is not to ask Jesus any questions unless you're sure that you want to cut to the center and *be* cut to the center by being forced to answer his questions in return. Those who broached some subject in order to test him or to justify themselves found that he was capable not only of dealing with the subject but also capable of turning the test around and of turning self-justification into soul-searching. Well does the book of Revelation describe Jesus: "In his right hand he held seven stars, and coming out of his mouth was a sharp double-edged sword. His face was like the sun shining in all its brilliance" (Rev. 1:16).

Nor is that brilliant sharpness reserved for people who didn't like him. We'll look next at the sharp questions he delivered to his own followers.

Questions for Reflection and Discussion

1. If Jesus were around today, what emotionally and politically sensitive questions might he have been asked to test him? What questions might he have used in response?

2. It's easy to see how *other people* are departing from the "spirit of the law" to search for loopholes. In what ways might you yourself be guilty of this?

3. I've said that the Pharisees wanted to teach ordinary people to bring holiness into everything that they did and every day of the week. Where then did the Pharisees go wrong, in the eyes of Jesus and the gospel writers?

4. In what ways do we have the "Christmas card list mentality" rather than that of "I'm available for whatever's needed"? Is "availability" practical in such a needy world?

Chapter Five

Rebuke by Question

Do you still not understand?
Where is your faith?

Jesus' Problems?

There is a peculiar passage in the eighth chapter of Mark's gospel in which Jesus heals a blind man. There's nothing strange about that, at least not in the context of a gospel. What's unusual is that Jesus seems unable to pull it off at the first attempt. Jesus spits in the man's eyes (which seems unnecessary to us, but was regarded as a reasonable treatment in those days), lays hands on him, and then asks, "Do you see anything?" The man replies, "I see people, but they look like trees walking around." After a second laying-on of hands, the man sees everything clearly.

This must rank as one of the strangest healings in the gospels. Why was he unable to get it right the first time? It's almost as if Jesus is a modern ophthalmologist, testing different prescriptions: "Now which one looks clearer, lens one or lens two?" Why did Jesus have such trouble with this particular healing? I hesitate to tell you that there might be more to this than meets the eye; but we'll return to this story in little while.

We've seen in a previous chapter that according to the gospels there are some things that Jesus doesn't know. Are there also some things that he cannot do—some phenomena that give him trouble? In this same chapter of the gospel, he also has a tough time getting his teaching through to his disciples.

Taking the Disciples Apart

I've kept a quotation from a student essay, because it contains just the right tone of ambiguity and accidental irony. "Jesus often takes the disciples apart to explain to them the meaning of some of his teachings." The writer was referring to Jesus' habit of telling parables to the crowds then explaining them to the disciples in private. But the ambiguity is correct: Jesus was not just "taking them aside," he was also "dismantling them" with his teachings. And it is clear that one of the ways he uses his questions is in a rebuking way, taking the disciples apart, dismantling them in the course of teaching them.

My sixth grade teacher comes back to my mind. He too had this ability to string questions together in a way that devastated the poor unfortunate at which they were aimed.

"Conrad! What do you think you're doing? Didn't you hear me tell the class to put their artwork away and get out their spelling? Are you deaf? Did you think I meant everyone but you?!" Bang, bang, bang; and with each "Yes, Mr. Davidovitch; No, Mr. Davidovitch," I felt more and more demoralized (though I'm sure I deserved it!).

There are no spelling books involved, but Jesus sometimes spoke to his pupils in an alarmingly similar manner: "Aware of their discussion, Jesus asked them, 'Why are you talking about having no bread? Do you still not see or understand? Are your hearts hardened? Do you have eyes but fail to see? And ears but fail to hear? . . . Don't you remember? When I broke the five loaves for the five thousand, how many basketfuls of pieces did you pick up? . . . When I broke the seven loaves for the four thousand, how many basketfuls . . . ?' He said to them, 'Do you still not understand?'" (Mark 8:17–21). Seven questions within the space of five verses—one after another: bang, bang, bang.

Has he lost his temper with them? He does seem awfully tired. He *has* just fed the four thousand; his opponents afterward *did* come up to him and, unreasonably, ask for a sign from heaven. At that, according to verse 12, he sighed deeply. Perhaps it's little wonder he is exasperated when even his followers are so worried about food that they cannot understand what he is saying. Is it irreverent to read this passage as Jesus expressing frustration?

In the middle of a story about exorcising a demon from a boy, Jesus interjects, "You unbelieving and perverse generation . . . how long shall I stay with you? How long shall I put up with you?" (Matt. 17:17 and parallels). Again, it looks to be the failing of his disciples that is the immediate cause of the outburst, though the saying is directed at the whole generation.

But Jesus' venting of frustration is different than ours. He never gives in to self-pity or gets paralyzed into giving up, but rather expresses his irritation and then gets on with things.

For he isn't merely inflicting his feelings on others. It is a genuine, if unpleasant, task of any teacher or parent to expose weaknesses, whether this is dressed in the language of "room for improvement" or, in more frank relationships, "this stinks." "Don't you understand this parable? How then will you understand any parable?" Jesus asked when the disciples missed the point of the parable of the Sower (Mark 4:13). He challenged them to get to grips with this story that would help them understand the rest of the stories.

I have great sympathy for the disciples, though. Knowing what we know now, it all looks so easy, but I can just imagine myself walking around in their sandals. How could I be expected to know when he was talking literally and when symbolically? When he tells me that these small five loaves are enough for the great crowd, he's talking literally, not figuratively. But when, a little later, he speaks of leavened bread again, he's talking figuratively, not literally. He says he's the bread, he says he's a gate, he says he'll have to be killed and then come back again. I'm sure I wouldn't have a clue what to think—my highest aspiration would be to follow and try to figure it out as I go.

Are You So Dull?

And Jesus is not just mysterious and symbolic; sometimes he's blunt to the point of almost rudeness, yet he expects his followers to get a serious message out of it. The discussion in Mark 7 starts because the disciples were eating without ritually washing their hands first. Although this was primarily ceremonial and does not necessarily mean that the disciples' hands were filthy or caked with germs, eating with unwashed hands would have been regarded as disgusting by those with delicate sensibilities: You want to be careful what you put into your digestive tract. Through the centuries we have become completely desensitized to Jesus' reply on this matter, despite the clear indicator in the parallel passage in Matthew that the Pharisees found his answer as disgusting as the disciples' practice. In an argument about food, cleanliness, and digestion, Jesus says, "Nothing outside you can defile you by going into you. Rather, it is what comes out of you that defiles you" (Mark 7:15–16). What would the hearers have thought he meant by "not what goes in, but what comes out"? Yrrg! If you or I were there, our jaws would drop. He *can't* mean what it sounds like he means! And no, he doesn't . . . or rather, doesn't *only* intend that meaning. He explains to the disciples: It's what comes out of a person's heart, not what goes in or out of a person's digestive system.

But while the symbolic interpretation is the only one we ever seem to consider today, the disciples evidently needed to be challenged to view it that way. They must have thought that he was talking only of digestive matters. "Are you so dull?" Jesus hits them with in verse 18. "Don't you see . . . ?" "Oh," they will have said, "Whew!"

It's understandable, but, yes, they *were* that dull, and a later book proves it. In verse 19, the writer of the gospel of Mark adds the comment, "In saying this, Jesus declared all foods clean." Yet Peter, who was there, didn't really embrace the implication of this for years. In Acts 10, Peter had a dream in which he was invited to eat nonkosher foods. Yet even so long after Jesus had died and risen, long after Pentecost, Peter's reply was, "I've never done such a thing. . . ." Now he was there when Jesus "declared all foods clean," indeed, many people think that Mark's gospel is based on Peter's remembrances. If so, mightn't the retelling of the gospel story be accompanied by a slap to the head with the heel of his palm? "Of course! How could I have been so dull? I didn't get it till Acts 10 but my master was saying this all along! In saying this, he declared all foods clean."

Where Is Your Faith?

On another occasion the disciples again run afoul of Jesus' mood and this time of the foul weather as well. This is the Calming of the Storm story, found in Matthew 8, Mark 4, and Luke 8. They're just sailing across the lake when the squall breaks out. Somehow, despite the commotion, Jesus has fallen asleep so that to get his help, the disciples have to wake him. He does help them—by having a word with the wind and waves. Literally, we're told he rebuked or scolded the storm! "*Bad* storm! Down, boy!"

Jesus also seems to rebuke the disciples, questioning their faith. Similar but different words are used in each of the three gospels in which the story appears. Mark has Jesus ask, "Why are you so afraid? Do you still have no faith?" Matthew has, "You of little faith, why are you so afraid?" while Luke has simply, "Where is your faith?" (The variations are easily explained by the different translations into Greek of the probably-Aramaic words of Jesus.) The disciples then famously ask each other, "What kind of man is this that even the winds and water obey him?"

But why was Jesus so hard on them? It's easy to dismiss the possibility that the storm wasn't that serious, that they were panicking without cause. These were experienced fishermen and dangerous squalls *can* arise without warning on these waters. The text clearly portrays a situation of real danger as well: The boat was being swamped.

The disciples could have done a lot worse. Mrs. Bayster, my old Sunday school teacher, always taught me that running to Jesus with my problems was a *good* thing to do. "What a friend we have in Jesus . . . all my sins and griefs to bear," we'd sing nearly every week. Would it not have been worse for them if they'd tried to deal with the storm using their own sailorly skills, without consulting Jesus? If he's grouchy after being woken up by his followers, what kind of mood would he have been in if their self-reliance had dumped him into the drink?

Perhaps they were supposed to have used their faith to calm the storm themselves. If you had faith the size of a small mustard seed, you could cause this mountain to be hurled into the sea . . . (Luke 17:6). That particular act would have made the sea even rougher, of course, but perhaps Jesus means that they should have been able to do what he did in calming it. It's possible, I guess.

Another solution that's sometimes proposed is that the disciples should simply have trusted that Jesus had greater things to do than be lost in a mere squall, thus God would have been watching over them and not letting them come to grief before "his time had come." I find this hard to accept as well. First, at this stage in the story, they've not really been introduced to the concept of Jesus' mission and destiny involving a necessary trip to Jerusalem and a stormy end there. More significantly, though, they seem to *already have had* the notion that God would protect him, so much so that Jesus has to rebuke them for *that*. When Jesus told Peter that his mission included going to Jerusalem to suffer and be put to death, Peter instantly responded, "Never, Lord!" (Matt. 16:21–22).

And yet, perhaps what is going on in the story is a combination of these two. They approach Jesus for help as the gospel writers probably think that they should. To that extent, they're doing the right thing. But in the story, they do so not with an attitude of faith, but with an attitude of panic. "We're going to drown!" Mark 4:38 goes so far as to have the disciples question Jesus' interest in them: "Don't you care if we drown?"

Faith is different from belief. Belief is impersonal assent, faith is trust. The disciples' defect is not the *belief* that the storm is deadly, nor the *belief* that Jesus could change things, as implied by their waking him and virtually blaming him. Their *beliefs* are in order. It is their *faith* that seems to have deserted them—their trust in and devotion to their master. Thus I think that answering "What should they have done?" with answers about their attitude toward the storm or themselves are answers that miss the point. The real problem is their attitude toward Jesus. "Don't you care about me at all?" is not a question you ask someone you're really connecting with, but rather a pretty good indicator that you're not as close as you could be.

Sharp or Abrasive?

This is a long way from the meek and mild Jesus that we've heard and read so much about. The usual antidote for the pale, anemic, agreeable, sentimental Jesus is to look at how he dealt with opponents, especially those money-changers in the Temple. Whip in hand, the outraged Jesus drove them forcibly out of his Father's House (John 2:15). But here we see him as abrasive or sharp even with his close friends, those whom he loved and who loved him enough to leave their nets and follow.

And perhaps it is more sharp than abrasive. Jesus is certainly not being difficult for the sake of it. Nor is it easy to believe that it is just a matter of him being grouchy because he got up on the wrong side of the boat. His sharpness underlines the miracle, and the result is that the disciples are shaken. My friend Steve Moody says that they are "shaken but not stirred" when they should have been "stirred and not shaken." They are not wounded by Jesus' words; his aim is not to punish them. They *are* shocked and astonished and we leave them considering "What manner of man is this?" He is tough on the disciples in order to prod them to do better. His remarks seem cutting, but they're probably best regarded as pruning—cutting back in order to stimulate growth. As we've seen with the parables, Jesus teaches by provoking people to reconsider their situations. "What kind of man is this?" The disciples are in a period of the gospel where they must consider this question carefully.

It won't be long before they'll be given their "mid-term exam," when Jesus will ask, "Who do you say that I am?" a question we'll discuss in more detail below.

The order and sequence is instructive. In Mark's gospel the disciples ask themselves, "What kind of man?" in Mark 4. But Mark 8 contains some of the other stories we've discussed. Chapter 8 contains the incident about bread in the boat—"Don't you remember? When I fed the five thousand. . . ? When I fed the four thousand. . . ? Do you still not understand?" And Mark 8 also contains the mid-term exam: "Who do you say that I am?" But, positioned right between those two incidents is the story with which we started. In between rebuking the disciples and asking them that central gospel question comes the story of the blind man: Jesus touches him once, and he's no longer blind, then touches him again to give him full and clear sight.

Perhaps the story is not about how Jesus had trouble healing some kinds of blindness but a deliberate comment on the disciples' own coming to full sight. The story of the two-stage gift of *eyesight* is the perfect introduction to that question about the extent of the disciples' *insight:* "Who do you say that I am?"

Questions for Reflection and Discussion

1. Can you recall times when someone used a series of rapid-fire questions to demoralize you? Can you recall other times when questions challenged you and spurred you to do better? What was different between the situations?

2. Students of the gospels sometimes use the phrase "acted parables" for actions such as when Jesus deliberately healed that blind man in two stages as a symbol for the disciples' two-stage understanding. Can you think of other "acted parables" from Bible stories or your own experience?

3. Was Jesus ever "rude" to anyone? Besides his comments about "coming out of a person" and the "cleansing of the Temple," what examples can you think of where Jesus was harsh with people?

4. Intellectually, we know that the "bungie cord" might be the right strength and length for the jump off of the bridge, but jumping is still something that we don't do easily. Can you think of more serious situations in your life where the difference between belief in something and faith in it were out of sync? How did you resolve the situation?

Chapter Six

Questions with No Obvious Answer

Why do you call me good?
Who do you say that I am?

An Irrelevant Reply

The gospels relate a story of a man who asked Jesus, "Good teacher . . . what must I do to inherit eternal life?" (Mark 10:17; Luke 18:18). Here, we might think, is a minor character who has his priorities right. He asks about eternity and he knows that Jesus is the right person to ask. Mark even tells us that he *ran* up to Jesus and fell on his knees before him. In that culture, both of these actions are indicative of someone humbling themselves. The dignified, important people would never be seen running or rushing anywhere, nor, of course, would they bend their knees to any other person but Herod or Caesar, and even then you can wager that they would not *fall* on their knees but execute a controlled and measured obeisance.

So how does Jesus react? Like a deep freeze at the outset! Hearing the man's question, Jesus seems to reply by first of all criticizing. It's not even the man's question he criticizes, but the greeting before it. And he seems to be nit-picking about technicalities. The man's approach was studded with interesting things that Jesus could have talked about: What does eternal life really mean? Is eternity time stretched on for infinity or a state outside of time? In what sense is eternal life, whatever it means, something that we "inherit"? Who has it now and where are they going that we might inherit it? And is one ever required to "do" anything in order to inherit? It should be, for Jesus, or any teacher of religion, a fascinating question, a worthy subject for a book in its own right.

But not Jesus. He begins by ignoring the man's question altogether and focusing on the greeting that precedes it. He objects to the perfectly ordinary word *good*. It is rather like writing, "Thank you very much for your letter of the twenty-first. You ask a great many interesting questions. But tell me, what *exactly* did you mean when you wrote 'Dear Sir'? 'Dear'? In what sense am I 'dear' to you? And the 'Sir' is similarly inappropriate. I am not a member of the aristocracy. And as for that comma...."

Jesus' reply to the man seems just as irrelevant and persnickety. Imagine your feelings: You've just run up to this great spiritual teacher, sliding the last few cubits on your knees, in order to ask about eternal life, and instead of answering you, it's as if he criticizes your grammar (and does so with a question, of course). "Why do you call me good?" Jesus answered. "No one is good—except God alone."

I imagine that Mr. Knees was just about to say, "Well, excuuse me. The jury is instructed to strike the word *good* from the record, Mr. Just-Slightly-Above-Average Teacher," and walk away disgusted. Before he can, however, Jesus seems to realize he's been abrupt, and mends his ways. This time, he answers precisely in his questioner's own terms, much to our surprise. We expected another question or at least a parable or something that would cause the man to redefine his question more in Jesus' terms. But no, Jesus trots out a list of the commandments. I challenge anyone today to line up a hundred Christians, selected on the basis of their proclivity to wear objects bearing the "What Would Jesus Do" slogan. Line them up and ask them, one by one, "What must I do to inherit eternal life?" If even one of them answered with the commandments, that would be remarkable.

But that's what Jesus does with this man, which plays right into his spiritual hands. "These things I have kept since I was a boy," he replies. And Jesus appears to believe him. The statement does not, of course, mean that the man thought himself perfect or without sin. Only God is *that* good. Judaism requires that you dedicate yourself to a way of life in which you keep the commandments in your heart, and follow the patterns of apology and forgiveness when you make mistakes in your attempt to live them out. The man is claiming precisely the same thing that Paul claimed when speaking about his years as a Jew: "As for the righteousness based on the law, faultless" (Phil. 3:6). Not sinless, but blameless within that system, which was, after all, God's system. That this is not mere prideful boasting on the man's part is clear from Jesus' attitude toward him in Mark. After he said he has kept these things since boyhood, Jesus looked at him and loved him.

Wait a minute, though. Did we say Jesus recited the Ten Commandments? Look again. There are some missing. Quite a few in fact. Some of the very first ones. In fact, all of the ones that have to do with a person's responsibilities to God are missing. How could Jesus have missed those?

Just One Thing?

But then Jesus says something that reminds me of a Monty Python skit. "There is one thing that you lack," he says. "Go sell everything you have. Give to the poor ... errr ... There are *two* things you lack: (1) Go sell everything you have, (2) Give to the poor so you have treasure in heaven, and (3) Come and foll ... uhh ... Three things ... you lack *three* things: (1) Go sell everything you have, (2) Give to the poor so that you have treasure in heaven, and (3) Come and follow me."

Jesus says there is one thing, then goes into a sequence of things. Is there one thing lacking or are there three? There is, in reality, only one thing. It is not a checklist of three requirements, like a shopping list or a three-fold path. It is, instead, a package, an attitude, a new perspective on the world that Jesus advocates—one that, for this man as for Peter and the other disciples, involves leaving everything behind in order to follow him. It's not the giving, it's not the selling, it's not even the *following* as an action. It is the devotion and reordering of priorities.

At this the man becomes very sad and walks away, because he was a man of great wealth. He had been able to manage a Checklist Spirituality, but the recentering of his life was something that he found too hard. In fact, as a good Jew, the man should have known something of this already, for neither are the commandments a checklist of ten things to be done one after the other. They were always intended as a covenant, Judaism as a whole God-centered way of life. As a checklist, even if you've kept them all from childhood but do not have God as the very center of your life, there is still one thing lacking. But now, astonishingly, Jesus is claiming that the one thing lacking is the placing of himself, Jesus, at the center, and as more important than the man's possessions and wealth.

And now, chillingly, we gain a different perspective on Jesus' apparently nit-picking question at the outset. The question that is so easily dismissed as irrelevant focuses on detail, "Why do you call me good?" That question is in fact *precisely* the answer to the man's question. "Good teacher, what must I do to inherit eternal life?" If he knows *why* it is right to kneel to Jesus, if he knows *why* it is *right* to call him "good," if he has come in order to follow, then he would have *had* the "one thing" which it turned out he lacked. And if he had that one thing, we could have skipped the talk about the commandments. Could this be the explanation for the missing commandments in Jesus' list? Is it that they are summarized in "Why do you call me good?" and following Jesus?

The odd thing, the paradoxical thing, is that although Jesus does say, "If you love me, you will obey what I command," it turns out that this will be no onerous chore. It turns out that, basically, what he commands is that people love him and follow him. So if you want to love him, you have to love him. If you want to follow him, you have to follow him. If you're doing it, you're already doing it.

Knowing why you call him good involves knowing who you think he is. As we will see shortly, this is precisely the question that Jesus fired point-blank at his disciples one day in a place called Caesarea Philippi.

Saying Good Things About Jesus

In medieval times, apparently, every monastery worth its marjoram simply *had* to have some sacred "relic" to venerate. An alleged piece of the cross was cool, but more common were bones of martyrs or gospel characters. I once heard of a wonderful French shrine which held a child's skull, maintained to be that of John the Baptist at age twelve. I'm not sure how they expected the poor guy to carry on after that age. Even in the first century, thirteen-year-old boys could be very cruel to school chums whose heads flopped around like rubber chickens. One rather suspects he would have acquired other nicknames than "the Baptist."

It has often seemed to me that a similar lack of common sense about "timing" haunts the thinking of the crowds in Jesus' day. When he asked his disciples, "Who do the crowds say that I am?" among the possibilities considered by the crowds is "John the Baptist returned from the dead." If it was reincarnation that they had in mind, Jesus would have had to have been born *after* John's death, one would have thought. Since Jesus' public ministry didn't really get going until John's imprisonment, though, the crowds may well not have known of Jesus' existence prior to John's death. It may have struck them as rational, then, that this new popular preacher might be John the Baptist resuscitated.

In any case, the crowds, as far as Peter is willing to tell Jesus, were thinking good things, even supernaturally good things, about Jesus: John the Baptist returned, Elijah returned, or some other prophet (Matt. 16:14; Mark 8:28; Luke 9:19). And although these are misleading views of who Jesus is, each has an element of the truth in it. Each would offer the gospel writers or Jesus an opening that any modern style politician or teacher would not be slow to exploit. "You might well think that I am a prophet for I have been sent by the big chief in the sky with a message for this people . . . ." a made-up Jesus might say. Or, "You are right to think of John the Baptist when you think of me, for John bore witness to me as the one who was to come." By now, I scarcely need to write that Jesus didn't do this, nor do I need to say what he did instead. He asked another question.

Messiah

"And what about you?" Jesus asks his disciples, leaving behind these great opportunities to preach, "Who do you say that I am?" Well, now, this is the question, isn't it? Remember, not very long ago at the calming of the storm they'd asked themselves a similar question in hushed voices so that their master wouldn't hear: "What kind of man is this?" Now Peter has to answer, face to face with the man. In all three gospels, he answers that Jesus is the Christ. This may not seem a remarkable reply to people nowadays—we almost regard Christ as Joseph and Mary's family name ("Mrs. Christ, can Jesus come out and play?"). It wasn't his last name, but a title.

Christ is merely the Greek for *Messiah*. Long exposure to the New Testament usage of the term for Jesus (after his time) has tended to blind us to the meaning that the word carried before and during his life. We tend to think that it was a Jewish "office," like President or Blackboard Monitor, whose duties were more or less spelled out ahead of time and that all that remained was sorting out who would be allowed to fill the position. It was nothing of the sort. While the Old Testament clearly points forward expectantly to dramatic events in the future, it turns out that *Messiah* is not one of the main categories or terms that it uses for this anticipation.

Nor is it a term that Jesus regularly uses for himself or his ministry. In fact, in the three gospels in which this story appears, Jesus never uses the term of himself before it, although the gospel writer—the narrator—does, as in Mark 1:1, "The beginning of the gospel of Jesus Christ" (NASB). When talking about himself, Jesus more frequently used another title, "son of man," which had a bit of ambiguity to it. It could be interpreted as the supernatural figure to which the Jewish prophet Daniel referred (Dan. 3:25), or it could have been just a generic term for "an ordinary guy," which appears to be its meaning in Psalm 8:4, "What is man that you care for him, the son of man that you think of him?" (NIV), Psalm 144:3, or any of a number of references in the prophet Ezekiel (2:1, 3, 6, 8; 3:1, 3, 4, 10, 17, 25ff).

In any case, Peter's answer of "Christ" is not presented by the gospels as the answer Jesus *taught* the disciples to give. Peter is not merely remembering and repeating the teaching he'd been given. There was no obvious answer to Jesus' question. With the benefit of two thousand years of hindsight, there are probably other answers with which Jesus would have been just as happy, and other answers which he may even have liked better. Peter was forced to come up with his own summary, based on what he'd seen and heard. That is why it is often called "Peter's Confession"—not "confession" in the sense that he admits he was wrong, but in the older sense of the word, which means acknowledging something, especially a summary of your beliefs or actions (whether good *or* bad) as your own.

Anointed for a Task

Literally, *messiah* means "anointed." In the Old Testament, an anointed person is one "chosen for a task." This begs the question "What task?" and the answer varies. For instance, although the Old Testament phrase "the Lord's anointed" often refers to the king, "anointed" is also used of prophets or workmen or even foreign leaders whom God happens to choose for particular tasks. A reasonable, if mundane, translation would be "appointee" or "nominee," which again clearly begs the question, "Appointed/nominated to what position or for what job?"

The early Christians' assertion that "Jesus is the Christ" could therefore be translated as "Jesus is anointed." It's a bit like the modern "Jesus is the Answer" where the obvious rejoinder is "But what's the question?" In first-century terms you'd reply, "But anointed for what task?"

Peter applied this term to the man he has been following. He saw it as a greater title than "prophet" (which the people had been willing to call Jesus). If, for Peter, a prophet is a person specifically called by God and given the task of bringing God's very words to the people, how does this status of Jesus as God's Appointee go further than that? What will a "Messiah" look like that goes beyond even the office of God's spokesperson and representative?

If people in Jesus' day had a view of what Messiah would be, it was not because they felt that they understood Old Testament teaching about a title, but because they felt that they understood the challenge and task that faced their generation. For many of God's people in the first century A.D., there was one task or question that must, they figured, have been uppermost on God's mind: freeing the land from the occupying forces of pagan Rome and restoring a godly and God-honoring rule to the people of God. Messiah, it seemed to them, would be given the honorable task of anointing Romans hard on the head with a blunt instrument. They trusted that the God who dealt with Pharaoh would raise up someone to deal with Caesar. It was not that they had meditated on and studied the concept of "appointee" or "candidate" in the abstract, but rather that each of the different factions felt that their intimate knowledge of the job description meant that they knew what the Appointee or Candidate would be like.

And so, Jesus as Messiah is a difficult but important insight. For the gospel writers, Jesus is not merely a prophet, but rather the one that prophets looked forward to. God's Prophet primarily brings God's message in words; God's Appointee was thought to enforce and carry out God's will via actions. This is why Peter was so stunned later in the exchange when Jesus predicted his own rejection and suffering at the hands of Jewish leaders. Peter would not have said, "Never, Lord" (Matt. 16:22; cf. Mark 8:32), so incredulously if it was Jesus *the Prophet* who would receive such treatment. This was thought to be *typical* treatment for a prophet bringing God's word to a deficient Jewish society (Matt. 5:12; 23:29–31, 37; Luke 6:23; 11:48–50; 13:34). God's Appointee, by contrast, would be a man of action who worked on behalf of an oppressed Jewish nation. How could the nation go against him? How could he fail?

Jesus As Doer

Peter realizes then that Jesus is not primarily a Teacher, bringing God's word (in which case Prophet would be an appropriate designation). Instead, he sees Jesus primarily as a Doer, fulfilling God's plans.

In the exchange that follows in Mark's and Matthew's accounts, it becomes clear that Peter does not understand all that Jesus understands about what being God's Appointee will involve. He sees but does not see. Rather like the blind man we've already mentioned, he sees men walking about like trees (Mark 8:24) and needs a further touch of Jesus before he will see more clearly.

Answering this question of Jesus' marks a real turning point for Peter, for the disciples, and apparently for Jesus as well. One part of the real task is finished; from this point forward, Jesus sets his face in a new way toward the rejection that awaits him in Jerusalem.

Other than their passages about Jesus' crucifixion and resurrection, there is arguably no more important passage than this for Matthew, Mark, Luke, or their readers. Whenever you find a commentary on one of these gospels that must be separated into two volumes, it is separated either before "Peter's Confession" or just after the Transfiguration story that is linked to it. Whenever someone produces a theatrical production based on one of these gospels, you'll find the major intermission comes at this point. This is the hinge on which the whole structure of the gospel swings, and it arrives not in the form of declaration, but in the form of a question: "Who do you say that I am?"

Jesus requires an answer to the question "Who do you say that I am?" and it isn't an obvious answer. At least it's not an answer that he has taught even the disciples to say in so many words. And following him is not primarily about intellectually grasping the answer (although, in the long run that's desirable), for Jesus is not primarily a teacher. Nor is following him primarily about obedience (although something like that will be required), for Jesus is not primarily a new law-giver. Primarily, it appears to be about your attitude toward him, from which obedience and understanding may begin to flow naturally.

Perhaps those hundred Christians with WWJD bracelets should trade them in. I advocate WDYSTIA armbands instead.

Questions for Reflection and Discussion

1. Like the rich young ruler in the story, people today tend to think that as long as you play nicely with everyone else, don't kill, don't steal, and so on, you're pretty well blameless. How does scriptural Judaism disagree with this? How does Christianity?

2. Although they don't regard the commandments as the basis of true religion, Christians obviously don't generally believe you can run around breaking the commandments. What do you think is the relationship between the attitude toward Jesus and any necessity of obedience?

3. Now, as then, the Middle East is full of different people groups with very different ideas about what the Big Task is. If a Messiah appeared in the Middle East today, what groups would claim him or her and how would each group see the Task?

4. Today, who do people say Jesus is? How does your view differ?

Chapter Seven

Jesus Pretends

What things . . . ?

No Gentiles Allowed?

A curious event took place when Jesus visited the non-Jewish region of Tyre and Sidon. A Gentile woman came to him and pleaded with him on behalf of her daughter, whom she was sure Jesus could help. His reaction, though typical and appropriate at the time and in that culture, shocks us: He says no. In Matthew's gospel, Jesus, like his disciples, seems to be of the opinion that she should be sent away. "I was sent only to the lost sheep of Israel," he says to them—only to Jews. It is remarkable that Christians should have such a saying of Jesus in their Bibles nowadays when most Christians are Gentiles. Jesus has said that he has *not* come for them.

But does he mean it, or is he offering the disciples an opportunity to dispute that statement? If he means it, why has he led them into Gentile lands?

That's Matthew's gospel. The writer of Luke's gospel, however, tells his tale in such a way as to make it clear that Jesus, despite everyone's initial expectations, had not come *just* for Jews. His gospel begins like some 1950s Hollywood musical with the characters constantly breaking into song, or at least psalm. Time after time, to the tune of some orchestra lurking off-stage, Mary or Zechariah or other people deliver lyrics about "delivering *his people* from the hands of *their* enemies." Even when Simeon sings about Gentiles, it is with all the empathy of telling them that God is going to teach them a lesson they'll never forget! "For my eyes have seen your salvation, which you have prepared in the sight of all people, a light for revelation to the Gentiles, and the glory of your people Israel" (Luke 2:30–32). Note: Israel gets the glory. It will be a "revelation" to everyone else, but they will see it all being prepared. This is a musical with a political message— a message about the people of Israel receiving *their* Messiah.

That's the attitude with which Luke's gospel *begins*. But then Luke does a curious thing. He does not tell the story of the *ministry* of Jesus from its beginning, but starts part of the way in. Other gospels tell us about Jesus teaching and healing round and about Capernaum. Luke just whooshes past that whole period like it didn't happen and goes directly from the baptism/temptation narrative to the sermon in his hometown, Nazareth. Mind you, he *knows* about Jesus' time in Capernaum. He even has Jesus refer to it (Luke 4:23) within the Nazareth story. But Luke jumps here in order to make the point unambiguously that from the earliest points in his public career, Jesus spoke about ministry not just to Jews but also to Gentiles. For, as part of this episode, Jesus winds up alienating his townspeople by talking about how great prophets like Elijah and Elisha did great things for non-Jews—that their ministry was not only for Israel. In fact, in this sermon he particularly calls attention to how Elijah helped *a Gentile woman and her child* in the region of Sidon. This in a sermon near the beginning of Jesus' ministry.

Yet Matthew's Jesus, fifteen chapters into the book, is still telling his closest followers that he was sent only to people within Israel—that he was not going to help *this* Gentile woman and her child. And it gets worse before it gets better. When, somehow, the woman actually does get through to confront Jesus directly, he slings the usual insult for Gentiles like herself, referring to her and people like her as *dogs*. She has asked for his help. "It is not right," Jesus replies, "to take the children's bread and toss it to the dogs."

The Master at Chess

Perhaps Jesus' words are the equivalent of a common chess strategy—a pawn offered to your opponent. Its capture leaves you with a disadvantage in terms of material, but gives you a positional advantage that more than compensates. This is a gambit, sending a piece out unprotected in the very hope that it will be seized. Your intention is to lose it.

Jesus played chess. Well, he did with his teaching, anyway. Even in Matthew's gospel itself there are other stories about Jesus helping Gentiles, suggesting that his statements to the disciples and to this Gentile woman do not truly represent his attitude toward non-Jews. It is Matthew, in fact, who tells us about the visit of the three Gentile wise men to Mary and Joseph's baby boy (Matt. 2:1–12). Matthew also tells us of people healed by Jesus in the Gentile region of the Gadarene (8:28–34) and, perhaps best of all, the cure of the servant of the Roman centurion in 8:5–13. In that story as here, a Gentile asks for help, not for himself but for someone in his charge. One might have mistaken a Syro-Phoenecian woman for a Jewish one, but it would be hard to mistake the centurion for anything other than a Gentile. Of him, Jesus winds up saying, "I have not found anyone in Israel with such great faith," and it is to his own followers that he says this (Matt. 8:10). Did Jesus intend the disciples to remember such incidents when he said to them, "I was sent only to the lost sheep of Israel"? Could it be that he was deliberately saying something that was not quite the truth in order to teach them to contradict it and their own biases? Could Jesus have been playing pawn to queen's bishop four?

It is no coincidence that he also uses the word *great* for the faith of this woman, also a Gentile (Matt. 15:28). Non-Jewishness is not the only thing that the woman and the centurion have in common. They are also marked as people who know how to answer Jesus. If Jesus was a man of questions, one thing that he loved was people who knew how to answer.

Back in Matthew 8, the centurion's faith was commended after his famous answer: He said that he was a man well accustomed to authority, giving and taking orders all day long, and he inferred that Jesus' miraculous authority must work along the same lines—Jesus' authority cannot be inferior to his own. The woman gives a similarly clever reply in her encounter with Jesus. And it is all the more remarkable in her situation.

How would you have felt? You've heard about this man; would you approach him? Is he your last hope? His followers, it's clear, want you to be sent away. But you battle on and manage to make it through to present your request, contritely, on bended knee to the man of wonders—to the man you hope will have compassion. But, disappointingly, he seems like all the rest. He too is dismissive and even implies that you're a dog and to help you would be like wasting food. "It is not right," he says to you. Will you argue with him?

The God Who Loves Debate

The God of the Jews and Christians is unlike any other god. Dispute with Jupiter and you'll have one of those yellow-painted wooden lightning bolts shoved down your throat. Talking back to Allah is likely to get you into even more trouble than talking back to my sixth-grade teacher, Mr. Davidovitch. Try arguing with Buddha and he'll laugh at you derisively for treating any conversation as if it referred to something real. But when you start arguing with Yahweh, he smiles, rolls up his anthropomorphic sleeves, and starts to look interested.

The strangest thing is that he likes losing the arguments even more than he likes winning them. Jacob, the trickster, is beloved of God. And Abraham didn't just get away with asking, "What about if there are only twenty righteous men in the city?" The God of the Jews and Christians is the only God that allows his followers to hear him say, "Oh, all right, you win."

The Jewish rabbis remember this even if the Christians forget. One of the best stories in the rabbinic literature concerns a great argument between some of the most illustrious rabbis in history, who could not agree with each other. Back and forth they went, each of the four or five sides in the dispute citing Scripture snippets to refute whatever had just been proposed. One of the rabbis, Eliezer, appealed to God to intervene in the dispute and, indeed, the Lord spoke from heaven saying loud and clear (and presumably in a Brooklyn Jewish accent), "Why are you fighting with Rabbi Eliezer? He is utterly and completely right!" This did not settle the argument as far as the other rabbis were concerned, however. One of them quickly cited Deuteronomy 30:12, "It is not in heaven," and interpreted it thus, "The Law has been given once for all at Mount Sinai; we do not listen to voices from heaven." And so it was that Rabbi Eliezer lost the argument despite having God on his side. Later, the story goes, one of the rabbis met Elijah and asked him how God felt about the whole business. Elijah related that God was laughing and shaking his head, saying, "My children have defeated me; my children have defeated me!"

And therein lies the key. Like any parent, God loves playing alongside his children. And like any parent, he loves it best of all when the little ones manage to do something to surprise him and win.

Rudeness As Provocation

And so with the Syro-Phoenecian woman. She argues. She replies to Jesus' gambit, not accepting it as his final word.

Jesus Asked

Jesus was more of a coach than a tutor; he was a motivator. From all of the evidence we have, he was superb at gauging where people were at, what they were thinking, and what they were capable of. And he used this knowledge not to make them all feel comfortable, but to prod and stretch them. Not everyone agrees with this interpretation of Jesus' motives—and his motives are not always easy to discern. It is true that throughout the New Testament the principle of "to the Jews first and *then* to the Gentiles" is an important one (cf. Paul's mission practice throughout Acts 13–20). But I find it difficult to believe that Jesus really intended to be rude to this woman and exclude her. If he held back, perhaps it was because he hoped that she would push. And he knew that effort on her part would force her to take him more seriously.

So how does she reply? She says, "Yes, Lord, but even dogs may eat the crumbs that fall from the master's table." A female talking back to a male, a Gentile to a Jew!

How his rejoinder then, and the smile that will have accompanied it, must have dissolved the tense atmosphere in that interchange. He commends her: "Woman, you have great faith." Not very many people heard that from Jesus' lips. That very hour her request was granted. Great faith, not little. She's no dog. Or at least, she didn't roll over and play dead.

When Jesus was rude to the Jewish religious big wheels, was he trying to provoke just such a response? Did he expect great things from them? When he had told the disciples he was only going to Israel, did he expect them to know better?

In the very next chapter of the gospel, Jesus tells his followers that he's bringing this generation no great sign, except the sign of Jonah. We chiefly remember Jonah for the three days in a great fish bit, but to the Jews, the book of Jonah is more than that. It is an object lesson. Its message is that you must not refuse to go to the Gentiles. We are told in the story of the Syro-Phoenecian woman that the people Jesus then encountered "praised the God of Israel" (Matt. 15:31). The fact that it doesn't simply say "praised God" is probably meant to imply that these were non-Jews praising a deity who had previously not been their God.

Jesus provoked the disciples and this woman, even if not as playfully as when he pretended to the disciples on the Emmaus Road, the story to which we now turn.

Written for Enjoyment?

Of all the questions that Jesus asked, I have no hesitation about which one is my favorite. It comes in a story told by Luke, an author with a wry sense of humor. Scholars, ever slow to get a joke, have only recently woken up to that fact. A recent book written on Luke and Acts was called *Profit with Delight*. For some people, the humor, action, and adventure in Luke's writing signals that his two-volume work was written for enjoyment. And this, for some, means it is more likely to be a novel, a type of fiction, than intended as a serious and factual history. Like many scholarly theories, though, this movement is right in what it affirms and wrong in what it denies.

Those of us who are academics by trade seem unable to remember that there is no international treaty requiring faithful histories to be dull, for some things *can be* entertaining and true at the same time. In the wider world, most normal people are aware that what really happens is very often funnier than anything an author could make up.

The title of the book *Profit with Delight* was inspired by the ancient author Horace, who used the phrase to describe the fictional adventure story. Closer to Luke's own time, however, the historian Polybius used *exactly* the same phrase, "profit with delight," to describe the goals of a writer of *history,* as a classics scholar has recently pointed out. So the fact that Luke tells his stories with some humor need not exclude them from the category of history, at least as the people of his time understood it.

A Practical Joke

The Emmaus story is told in the twenty-fourth chapter of Luke's gospel. It is a few days after the crucifixion when two disciples meet who they think is a stranger on the road. This stranger is, though they don't know it at first, the resurrected Jesus. And in this story their master does something extremely odd: He "misleads" them. He plays something of a practical joke on them!

When he approached them on the road, they were vexed by Jesus' death. Luke tells us that they were not only talking about the recent events, but they were also arguing with each other about them. Before his death, Jesus had spoken to the disciples about his suffering and death; but as we've seen earlier in this book, he often spoke in riddles and you could never take it for granted that the words he said should be accepted at face value. So they talked and argued about whether Jesus *meant* for all this to happen, or whether he merely predicted the inevitable. What would Jesus or the Father want them to do now to carry on his work? Could they even try?

Now joining them on the road is the one person who can answer their questions and settle their arguments. And what does he do? He *pretends* not to know what they are talking about! Irreverent as it may be, I cannot help but think of Bugs Bunny. Here's old Elmer Fudd, a huge floppy hunting cap on his bald head, shotgun in hand, sneaking along on tiptoe. Soon he passes Bugs, leaning casually against a tree, munching noisily: "Eh, what's up, Doc?" Elmer, somehow, doesn't recognize Bugs, and puts a finger to his lips: "Be vewy, vewy quiet," he says in a stage whisper. "I'm hunting wabbits!"

Luke tells us nothing one way or the other about carrots, but you can almost hear a Fudd-like consternation when the disciples ask their innocent-looking companion, "Are you the only visitor to Jerusalem who does not know of the things that have happened there in the last few days?!" Then comes my favorite of all Jesus' questions. You'll know by now that it isn't unusual for Jesus to answer a question with a question, but never have we heard such a surprising one as this, nor one delivered with such a twinkle in his eyes. They ask, "Are you the only visitor to Jerusalem who does not know of these things?" And the Lord Jesus looks at them with wide eyes and asks, "What things?" Eh, what things, Doc?

Most of us don't usually think of Jesus Christ as the kind of guy who would pull people's legs, and perhaps I run the risk of offending some people by putting it this way. But I'm afraid the ancient text leaves us no way around it. When it comes to things like the trial and resurrection, he knows about the events better than they do. Yet he kids them: He pretends not to know. He feigns ignorance so that they will explain their perceptions of the events to him.

The text even uses the word *pretend (prospoieō)* later on in the story. Even after talking together with this "stranger" about the events and their significance in the Scriptures, the disciples do not recognize him, and in verse 28, he "pretends" to be traveling further. This forces the disciples to plead with him. Eventually Jesus allows himself to be persuaded to do what he secretly must have intended to do all along: that is, to stay with the disciples and share with them further.

Neither Mere Amusement Nor Teaching Opportunity

Jesus pretends! How can this be? What can he have in mind? To be sure, if this is practical joking, it is not merely for amusement's sake. He is doing more than just giving evidence of a playful disposition, though there may well be something to that effect as well, as C. S. Lewis imagines in *The Lion, the Witch and the Wardrobe*. In that book, the character Aslan becomes a bit friskier after *his* resurrection: "Oh, children," said the Lion, "I feel my strength coming back to me. Oh, children, catch me if you can!" And there followed chasing and laughing and tumbling so that Lewis writes, "Whether it was more like playing with a thunderstorm or playing with a kitten Lucy could never quite make up her mind." Perhaps the Jesus who displayed human emotions in the Garden of Gethsemane before his torture and crucifixion, also displays a certain dose of relief and playfulness after the resurrection. But that's not all there is to this story.

Jesus' pretense is not primarily intended to give an occasion for him to teach the disciples, though he does take advantage of the opportunity. He asks, "What things?" and they inform the stranger, giving a rough account of what had been going on. Their story is left hanging in a very open-ended manner. The disciples have not had their high expectations met, but neither have they completely lost sight. They say, "but we had hoped that he was the one," as if it was clear to them now that he was not who they had thought. Yet they recount the mounting evidence for the resurrection as if they don't know what to make of it. That "the Lord is alive again" looms as a mysterious possibility in their retelling.

Jesus rebukes them, gently. Then he asks them another question: "Was it not necessary for the Christ to suffer these things and to enter into his glory?" Probably without leaving them an opening big enough to say, "um . . ." he explains to them how, from start to finish, the Scriptures declare that it *was* necessary. Incredibly, according to Luke, while on the road, Jesus manages to interpret the entire sweep of the Old Testament in terms of himself and his mission. How we would love to have the text of that teaching session! And the disciples, looking back on the episode some time later, remember this time, "Were not our hearts burning within us while he spoke to us on the way?"

One of the biggest and best surprises in the whole story is *what doesn't happen* after Jesus' teaching. If you or I were making up such a story, there would be no question about what would happen next. With their divine Tutor beside them, having just demonstrated so dramatically his ability to teach and interpret Scripture, the disciples would have their eyes opened and they'd realize who this stranger really was. This is the Divine Revealer of Truth. This stranger rebukes, he asks questions, and he teaches with authority. This is our Master.

But this is not what happens. Surprising as it is, that is *not* how they recognize him. They take it all in as best they can, but the pretense continues. So even after he expounds the Scriptures to them on the road and they listen with eager and innocent ears—even then—Jesus pretends. He finally pretends to allow himself to be convinced not to go further but to stay and have supper with them.

Recognition At Last

They do eventually recognize the "disguised" Jesus. But it is not the walking with them that does it; it's not the asking of questions (as characteristic as I've made that out to be); it's not even the comprehensive and insightful teaching. It is only when the stranger/guest assumes the role of host at the meal and performs four actions, that the disciples wake from their stupor. They didn't know him for who he was when he rebuked and asked and taught. But everything is different when he *takes* the bread, *gives* thanks, *breaks* it, and then *gives* it to them.

This very set of actions is also present, among other places, in the accounts of the miraculous feedings and then again, more recently, in the accounts of the Lord's Supper.

He *took* bread, *gave* thanks, *broke* it, and *gave* it to them. To those who knew him, *this* was even more characteristically and unmistakably Jesus than what had happened on the road, although now they also can see how obvious it should have been before: "Didn't our hearts burn within us?"

It is through fellowship with him, letting him be the one who serves, letting him be the host, that the connection is made. And this once again reinforces the idea present throughout the gospels: Jesus is not remembered primarily because he was a Great Teacher, but primarily because of what he took up and allowed to be broken. The Lord's Supper, not the Sermon on the Mount, is the centerpiece of the gospel story. But then again, perhaps it *is* precisely the role of a good teacher to share of himself, and it is our notion of a teacher primarily as "all-knowing explainer" that is at fault.

In the course of this chapter we have seen some people who knew how to answer Jesus' questions. There is a right way and a wrong way. The subject of the next chapter is how *not* to answer his questions.

Questions for Reflection and Discussion

1. Put yourself in the disciples' sandals. If you had been a Jew in the first century, you too would have had trouble with the idea that God wanted to help non-Jews. Why? What kinds of things that Jesus did and said might have changed your mind?

2. I've claimed that the Judeo-Christian God loves to argue and doesn't even have to win to enjoy it. Does this ring true with you, or have I overstated the case?

3. In the story of the road to Emmaus, Jesus' sacrificial giving is emphasized, shown to be more important than even his teaching. Is this characteristic or uncharacteristic of the Bible? Of the church? Of your spiritual life?

4. The same Jesus who said, "Let your yes mean yes and your no mean no" (Matt. 5:37, translation mine), also "pretended" (Luke 24:19, 28). Clearly, there must be some difference between "pretending" to other people and lying. What might those differences be and what are the implications for our own speaking and acting?

Chapter Eight

How Not to Answer Jesus' Questions

Neither will I tell you . . .

An Ambiguous Title

I don't remember where—somewhere where English isn't the first language like Switzerland or Romania or a breakfast place in central London—but I once saw a sign that read "No-smoking is permitted." The intriguing thing is that without the hyphen, the meaning seems clear: "No smoking is permitted" means the same thing as "Smoking is not permitted"—no instance of the behavior, smoking, is allowed. *With* the hyphen there, however, the ambiguity of the sentence is highlighted. Although none of the words have changed, the small addition of the hyphen means that the text should really be read as the behavior of "no-smoking" will be permitted. Nothing is said about the behavior of "smoking" and whether or not that is also permitted. It reminds me of the time some cartoon-strip character defended himself to the policeman: "But officer, the sign said that this spot was *Fine* For Parking!"

Sometimes being able to take something two different ways is an advantage. You want to say both things at once. I was told of one academic who reviewed a book with which he disagreed. He knew he would assign it to all his students, to teach them to refute it. He wrote his review, and was quoted on the back cover: "This is an incredible resource for students." He meant, of course, not that it was incredibly good but that it had no credibility.

The title of this chapter is offered up in that spirit of ambiguity! On the one hand, it might be read: "What you must not do when you're trying to answer Jesus' questions." On the other, it might also be rendered: "How to sidestep Jesus' questions." In a way, this chapter will be about both of those things.

But asking about the truth must be good and noble; why would anyone *avoid* answering Jesus' questions? Two reasons: inconvenience and self-image. Difficult questions are, well, difficult. Just think about diet or exercise or ethical investing. You know what's good for you and what will feel great in the long term, but that's no guarantee you can face up to the short-term pain. It takes a lot of energy to answer hard questions, and may take even more to work through and change your life according to what you find. And on top of the possibility of having to change, you may also need to acknowledge that up till now, you have been wrong. It should come as no surprise that many people who hear the questions of Jesus wish they hadn't. In a way, this chapter will be about both of those things.

If We Say This, He'll Say That

Earlier in the book, we looked at a story from Luke 20 in which Jesus was asked, essentially, "Who said you could do this?" If someone wheeled in a wooden cart and started selling farm-grown produce near the main entrance of your supermarket, it wouldn't be long before some store manager came out and asked, "Who gave you permission do this?" The chief priests were similarly protective of the teaching in the Temple.

But as we've seen, instead of answering, Jesus asked a deceptively similar question back. He asked about John the Baptist. Interestingly, Jesus had another possible tactic that he did not take. In the gospels, he does *not* ask, "Did you give permission for J. the B. to do what he did?" When they answered "no," Jesus could then have said, "Neither do I need your permission." Instead his question is whether John operated under the authority of human beings or under the authority of God. He wanted to set up a contrast between those two types of authority. Through the choice of tactic, between the lines of his questions he is saying something about the possibilities of *his authority* rather than merely proving *his independence* from the institutions and authorities of his day.

Jesus' question is brilliant, but for the purpose of *this* chapter, the most significant thing is the answer that Jesus received. Or rather, even more important is the method by which the chiefs and elders come up with their answer. Their answer, you may remember, was, "We don't know." They claim they don't know whether they think John's message was of earthly or heavenly origin. Religion is their job; John the Baptist was obviously a religious (although also a political) figure. Is it really credible that they should not have an opinion on this matter?

When they discuss the question among themselves, it is striking that they do not ask themselves about John or his work and message at all. You'd think that they would.

Earlier I compared their method of deliberation with my own chess-playing calculations. "If I go here, he goes there, I take that, he takes that; no, that doesn't work." That's just how the big shots in the story act when they say: "If we say John's message was from heaven, he'll ask why we didn't follow him. But if we say his message was merely human, we'll get in trouble with the people." So, out loud, they answered, "We don't know."

They don't know because they haven't *tried* to face the question. They do not concern themselves with trying to come up with an answer that conforms to the truth of the matter; they instead concern themselves with forging an answer that avoids producing unpleasant consequences. Their first duty is not to the truth of the answer, but to the practical implications for themselves.

Virtually any reader today will connect the leaders' behavior with politicians even more strongly than with chess players, although the element of calculation links them both. Politicians in interviews tend to listen not for the questions, but for opportunities. They don't hear what you're asking but rather what they want to say—or rather what they want to be seen as saying. They have learned to concern themselves not with answering according to what they think is the reality, but according to what they judge will do them the most good. "Is software company X a monopoly that has harmed the public and reduced competition in the industry?" is a question that is sometimes answered not on the basis of the number of competitor word processors that have survived and are still on the market, but rather on the basis of tax and advertising revenue and campaign donations. Isn't this what Jesus called "pleasing people rather than God"?

So facing the question and simply ducking it isn't good enough. Jesus himself does that (although in the process, manages to signal the answer to any perceptive observers). Nor is giving no answer sufficient. Rather, the best way *not* to answer Jesus is to avoid even *facing* the question, at least on its own merits. Meditate on the effect that answering will have on you rather than on the subject matter at hand.

Last Time / This Time

We find another wonderful example of this behavior in the book of the Acts of the Apostles, Luke's sequel to his gospel. Chapters 3 and 4 relate an incident that takes place in the time after Jesus. Peter and John, Jesus' disciples, found themselves lacking ready cash when a handicapped beggar asked for change. So, they shrugged their shoulders, apologized, and healed the poor guy instead. But they did this in the Temple courts and that drew a crowd. Then (as in the story above from the gospels) they began to teach this crowd in the Temple—on the chief priests' turf. And we *know* how much the Temple bureaucrats smiled upon unplanned and unauthorized events like that!

Peter and John were arrested, spent the night in a jail, and in the morning were brought before the Splendid Masters of Jerusalem. First-century jails were not known for their comfortable sleeping quarters nor for the range of facilities for freshening up in the mornings. The writer means for us to notice the contrast between the wealthy and powerful Council members and the hungry, dirty, smelly Galilean prisoners.

There's another contrast that the author means for us to notice but which most readers do not. If this were a movie or a play or if the whole of Luke and Acts were read aloud to you (as was probably originally intended by the author), you wouldn't be able to avoid noticing the striking similarities and contrasts between this scene and one that happened at the end of the gospels. Peter has been to this building before. Last time, however, Jesus was on trial inside and a fearful Peter was cowering outside, making up lies because he was afraid of the High Priest's servant girl ("I tell you, I don't know him!" Luke 22:54–62). This time, it's Peter in the hot seat, face to face with the Big Cheese himself, not some chambermaid.

Now Peter and John were not arrested for being Christians; they had been arrested for causing a ruckus in the Temple and for teaching about the resurrection (which the Sadducees, the party most concerned with the Temple, did not believe in). The Council that morning had probably only been told about the unauthorized disturbance that Peter and John caused.

This helps to explain the gift of a straight-line that the High Priest blundered into handing to Peter. "By what power or name did you do this?" The question is just like that other question to Jesus in *his* lifetime. Essentially, it's the Big Guys asking the rebels, "Who said you could do this?"

The High Priest was not asking a *genuine* question to Peter here. It's like the time Mr. Davidovitch asked me, "Who exactly gave you permission to dangle the resuscitation dummy outside the third graders' window?" The Council thought they knew exactly how naughty little Peter would have to answer. The High Priest *is* the authority; it is *his* permission that these nobodies should have sought (albeit indirectly) before gathering such a crowd and preaching such messages in the Temple. According to the script, Peter *should* have crumpled at this point and stuttered, "Uh, no one, your excellency. No one gave me permission. A thousand pardons. It will not happen again." But, unwittingly, he handed Peter some beautiful openings. And (somewhat surprisingly when you remember his previous denial of Jesus in the courtyard) Peter used every single opportunity to the max just as his master Jesus might have.

Ooh, a Wise Guy, Eh?

Peter began by "creatively misunderstanding" the question put to him. When the High Priest asked, "By whose power or name did you do this?" what he'd meant by the word "this" was the *disturbance,* especially the gathering and teaching of the crowd. Peter, however, put on an innocent-looking face and answered instead, "By 'this,' perhaps you mean the healing of the lame man?"

Was this a *deliberate* misunderstanding? I think so. If it was, it is instructive to note how different Peter's cleverness was from the self-centered calculations of the leaders elsewhere. While it is true that he rearranged the question somewhat to fit the answer he wanted to give, he had no trouble meeting the heart of their question head-on. But then again, it might have been an unconscious reinterpretation of the question. What was important about the incident from the High Priest's perspective is not what is important from Peter's. From their clashing worldviews, when the Council looked at the situation, they saw one thing and Peter saw quite another.

As for the "Who said you could?" part of their question, the signature on the metaphorical dotted line was none other than Jesus'. And lest they think that this was not a very high authority, Peter told them that God had reversed their stated opinion of Jesus. The High Priest and his cronies had dismissed and killed him, but God, whom they cannot ignore, raised him from the dead. Not only did the disciples have Jesus' name on their hall pass/permission form, but, Peter argued, there is no other signature that would do the trick ("No other name given under heaven by which we must be saved," Acts 4:12).

. This must have offended the High Priest and his own sense of prestige. Rather than the sheepish "No one gave me permission, sir. It just happened" that he expected, he was suddenly confronted with a challenge to his own authority and to his previous decisions. No wonder that at this point they noted Peter's courage with surprise. The author also tells us that this is when they realized they were dealing with Christians (4:13).

Jesus Asked

Peter's creativity continues later as well. He has answered the "name" bit of "By what power and in whose name?" but he makes a play on words using "power" only later. Near the end of the story, the Council told Peter and John that they could go free if they kept quiet about the whole affair. Peter now admitted that he was "powerless." "I'll let you be the judges," he said (itself full of irony, since they were meant to be the Supreme Judges in Israel). "Judge for yourselves: is it right to obey you or God? We are powerless . . . powerless to do anything other than speak about what we have seen and heard." Such mischievous courage from one who cringed in the courtyard a few weeks before!

The Deliberations

But, clever as the antics of the good guys in the story are, they are not our primary interest here, but rather the cogitations of the bad guys. These holy men of Jerusalem have had some fairly remarkable events shoved into their pious faces. The lame walk and the uneducated answer back and confound the learned. Perhaps, worst of all, they are reminded of the rumors that their God has seen fit to reverse their judgment on Jesus, raising him from the dead. They *should,* you would think, discuss these remarkable reports. Could any of it be true? They might decide that it isn't—fair enough—but you'd think that they should at least stop, reconsider, and make that decision.

At the very least they should rethink their attitude toward these people. Did Peter and John *mean* to cause a disturbance? Are these Galileans guilty or innocent of causing a commotion in the Temple without a permit? They should stop, reconsider, and make a decision.

To a large extent, the language about "killing Christ" is precisely about the need to reconsider. When Peter brings up the fact that "they crucified Jesus," it isn't primarily in order to make them feel guilty, as many readers have assumed through the years. The "crucified" bit isn't the important part of the sentence. It's really about contrast: "You crucified him but God raised him." Several times early in the book of Acts, this is the point the Jewish disciples make to their fellow Jews. You killed him, but God raised him (Acts 4:10, as also 2:23–24 and 3:15). It's not about blaming them; rather, it's about the reversal. You said no, but God said yes. And that reversal should cause them to reconsider as thousands of people did in both chapters 2 and 3. You said no, then God said yes. Now what do you say? Think again!

In Acts 4:15–18, the court asks Peter and John to withdraw so the judges can confer. But as with Jesus' opponents earlier, they do not really confer at all. Their tragedy consists not so much in having crucified Jesus as in their refusing to reconsider now. The claims are not rejected, they just don't come up for discussion. The facts of the healing are taken note of only insofar as they affect public opinion. There is no attempt to explore whether the healing happened and what it might signify. Such things are not permitted to affect *what they think,* only *how* they might expediently *react*. They realize that they cannot enhance their credibility by denying this miracle (as seems to have been their first inclination), but if they tell their prisoners to keep quiet maybe it won't do them too much damage. And so, looking at chessboard Jerusalem, they calculate:

Jesus Asked

"We can't go there, or they'll go there. But if we stop that, then perhaps we can save this . . ."

Their response, again, is based not upon what is the truth of the matter but upon what serves them best in their struggle to preserve their own status and respectability. Their goal is to stop this from spreading. They are unwilling to talk about whether that is the right thing to want. They refuse to budge and decide to hold on, not reconsider. That is how not to answer Jesus.

Beyond Answering

Can't Jesus be accused of the same thing? We've spent most of the book enjoying how he parried questions, spent a whole chapter on how he sidestepped them, and even talked about him as resembling a chess player. Are these leaders any different from Jesus?

When we looked at the story about paying taxes to Caesar, the Show Me a Coin story, it was clear that in asking Jesus about taxes, his questioners were not really interested in knowing what Jesus thought or what to do about the taxes. They were not really asking, they were merely hoping to trap him.

In fact, although Jesus' replies are seldom what his questioners expected or hoped for, they seem always to show him as someone who has seen more deeply into the problem than the questioners have. Unlike the politicians' mode of operation, Jesus does not dismiss questions as inconvenient if they do not afford him an opportunity for self-advancement. Jesus dismisses questions, when he does so, in order to answer the deeper questions. As we've seen, faced with a question about his authority, Jesus shows the real issue to be about divine as opposed to earthly authority. Faced with a question about taxes, Jesus grounds it in ideas about creation. When he was asked about divorce, he chose instead to throw the spotlight on marriage.

When Jesus refused to answer the question put to him, it was frequently because the question wasn't the heart of the matter. His opponents usually asked without really asking just as they answered without ever answering. Jesus went beyond answering, or behind it, or somewhere else surprising, whereas the other guys simply stopped short.

Truth or Consequences

Refusing to allow the status quo to be questioned is not unusual. Such behavior is not limited to first-century big shots: I do it and you do it. We do it with each other and we each do it with ourselves. And we probably do it more with questions of responsibilities and religion than with questions about anything else. It's not only that we want to preserve the cozy equilibrium we've found, we also want to save face and not be shown to have been in the wrong.

What prevents most people from becoming genuine committed followers of Jesus of Nazareth today? It is not that they cannot find convincing rational answers to the hard questions like "If God is good, why is there evil?" or "Will a child who has never heard of the 'Good News' go to heaven or hell?" If you're like me, there are some things even harder than the intellectual difficulties of the faith. What's harder is knowing that my life would have to change if I believed it and guessing what might be said about me by people whose approval and respect I crave. Like the authorities in Luke's story, the answers to Jesus' questions are debated not on the grounds of what is true, but on the grounds of what "works for me" and causes the least disruption.

If we're going to handle his questions that way, we may as well know we're doing it. Here, then, is a simple guide as to How Not to Answer Jesus' Questions. Step One: Don't face the question, think your way all around it. Never mind "truth," think "consequences." Do Step One correctly, and you'll never need to worry about any Step Two.

In the final chapter we'll try to unearth why Jesus asked all these questions. What did he hope to learn by doing it? What is it he wanted to know?

Questions for Reflection and Discussion

1. Was there a time that you found yourself not facing someone's difficult questions? What brought about the necessary change in your attitude?

2. I've claimed that although Jesus sometimes didn't answer the question he was asked, with Jesus it was because he always went deeper, whereas his opponents stopped short. Was this a gift that he had or can we learn it? How might we cultivate it in ourselves?

3. How do you balance a willingness to tackle questions about the logic of the faith, such as "Why is there evil?" and about the dying child who hasn't heard the gospel, on the one hand with the real tendency people have to avoid the practical implications of coming to believe on the other?

4. In a very peculiar story in John 5:1–15, Jesus asked an invalid, "Do you want to get well?" I'm tempted to think his reply is a similar kind of avoidance, and I think the rest of the story bears me out. What do you think?

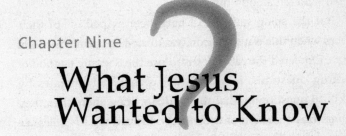

Chapter Nine

What Jesus Wanted to Know

What do you want me to do for you?

Those Poor Guys!

Jesus told lots of parables in the course of his career, and he also asked a lot of questions. You have to feel for the poor disciples. They would have cheered when Jesus launched questions against those they perceived as opponents. There might well have been smug smiles on their faces when Jesus met a minefield-like question like the one about taxes to Caesar with the coin trick and the barbed wire implications of "Give Caesar what is his and give God what is *his*." And it will have become clear to the astonished disciples that even apparent attempts to duck the questions of others became occasions for Jesus to ask questions that pierced to the hearts of issues. They will have listened with amazement as Jesus dissected the theology and practice of learned men with questions like "What did Moses *command* about divorce?" and "Which of these *became* a neighbor to the man who fell among thieves?"

But the smug smiles will have been wiped off of their faces when this water cannon was turned on them. We might have expected the rabbi Jesus to use the Socratic method of asking questions, in which the teacher demonstrates by skillful questioning that the students know more than they consciously *know* that they know. Instead the disciples are subjected to a torrent of questions not designed primarily around information as information at all. Instead, some were the questions of rebuke: "Do you still not understand?" and "Where is your faith?" Here, clearly, Jesus himself was not in the dark. He knew that they did not understand and their faith was missing in action. Neither was he asking in order to demonstrate to them that they knew. But such questions do have an effect on the questionees. They forced the disciples to admit something about themselves.

Perhaps the smugness returned when Jesus asked them questions with obvious answers, like "Which of the two sons did what the father required?" and "Which of the two debtors would be the more grateful?" Again, as with many of the parables, these questions did not so much have the effect of bringing preconscious *knowledge* to the surface as of forcing a conscious acknowledgement of a principle that would have a pointed application outside of the story.

But the disciples would have been in trouble again when faced with other questions that did not have obvious answers,

"Why do you call me good?" and "Who do you say that I am?" even though these performed much the same task: forcing a consciousness of their stance with regard to Jesus, rather than to a consciousness of any facts or knowledge or geometric principles.

Smugness might well have faded into confusion and stupefaction when Jesus told the foreign woman that it was not right for him to spend his energy on "dogs" or the time he pretended to the Emmaus travelers that he did not know about the events in Jerusalem and that he couldn't stop at their house. Again in these incidents, the transaction is not primarily one concerning information but concerns the position or attitude or allegiance of the person being questioned.

That's why avoiding Jesus' question is the best way to not answer it, as we saw in the previous chapter. Those who were best at not answering were those who thought their way all around the question and did not declare their stances on the central matter.

Now I don't *disagree* with the picture of the Jesus who called people saying, Follow me! I think he did things like that. He commanded disciples and got angry and turned over money changers' tables. But I would want to argue with a portrait of Jesus that sees him operating *exclusively* in Charisma and Command Mode. Evangelists are renowned for telling their audiences that "Jesus is the Answer." Well, who today wants to hear some guy still wearing a twentieth-century hairdo telling you what the Answer is? They might do better to say, "Jesus is the Question," which is just as true to the New Testament. Not "Now I'm going to *tell* you something," but Richie's "I wanna ask ya somethin'."

The Mystical Jesus

Another image this questioning dispels is the picture Mrs. Bayster perhaps inadvertently painted for me of a supernatural guru Jesus who does nothing but spooky, mystical things all day long. The story known as the Transfiguration is a prime example (Mark 9 and parallels). Jesus takes a couple of disciples up on a mountain. His face begins to shine and suddenly there are two old guys up there with him. Peter somehow recognizes these two as Moses and Elijah.

I've often wondered how he made that connection. Moses and Elijah are not like Churchill and Roosevelt. It's not like there was old newsreel footage of Old Testament characters that Peter would have seen on TV hundreds of times. You see two old guys on a mountain top, right? Even if they glow, are you going to think they must be Old Testament folks from thousands of years in the past or are you going to think, *Why are those two geezers glowing like that?* And why does Peter recognize them as those particular two Old Testament guys? How in the world does he know that they're not Adam and Samuel or King David and the prophet Isaiah? Maybe they wear name badges in heaven: "Hello, my name is—Moses. Have a nice day!" In any case, although Jesus does do some things that are supernatural and difficult to understand, we often think of the Jesus of the gospels this way *only,* as if he were constantly or exclusively doing mysterious things beyond our comprehension, as if the weird stuff was all there was to him.

Jesus of the Straight Answer

It therefore takes us off guard when he acts in a way that we would consider as normal. After all these stories about other people's traps and Jesus' cleverness, Mark 12:28–34 is disarming in its simplicity. I hope you're sitting down, because this is going to shock you: Someone asks Jesus a question and—get this—he *answers* it!

The story starts with the two main "denominations" of Jews in the first century, the Sadducees who do not believe in a life after death and the Pharisees who do. Jesus has just completely stumped a crowd of objecting Sadducees with one of his unanswerable "Have you not read . . . ?" questions. He ended the harangue with the words "You are badly mistaken!" The Pharisees were impressed with how he silenced their Sadducean rivals. So one of the Pharisees asked him about the greatest commandment in the law.

The summary Jesus gives is deservedly famous, although it is probably not a formulation that he himself invented: "Love the Lord your God with all your heart and with all your soul and with all your mind and with all your strength." For once, the questioner is not left speechless and astonished.

The two of them resemble jazz musicians swapping solos. The man replies, "Well said!" (that's "AW-right! Yeah!" in the original Aramaic) and proceeds to crank out a variation on the theme involving the superiority of devotion over sacrifice. Jesus returns the compliment: "You are not far from the kingdom of God." The phrase is tantalizing. Does he mean "close" as in "the kingdom of God is close at hand and you're in"? Or "close" as in "close but no water-cooled pipe"? In any case, here was a questioner who appears to really have wanted to hear. To such people, Jesus *could* give a straight answer.

Whatcha Got?

And there are other, more surprising occasions of ordinariness. Just after that wonderful incident in Emmaus, Luke tells another story about the resurrected Jesus (Luke 24:36–49). In this story, the question he asks is again priceless. Picture the scene: The disciples are still frightened about the authorities—if their leader could be arrested and executed, they too could be in serious trouble. Suddenly Jesus himself appears among them. The dead man is there and apparently alive. He tells them not to be afraid and then tries to prove that it's really him. And then the text says, "While they were still having trouble believing it in their joy and amazement, he asked them, 'Got anything to eat around here?'" How's that for being disarmingly ordinary? Raised from the dead and he's interested in what's cooking.

Of course, it's not mere hunger that stands behind the question. If they're thinking that his appearance might be that of a ghost, one of the best ways to counter that is by performing a bodily function like eating. In the Emmaus story, you'll remember, Jesus disappears from the house of the two disciples after taking the bread, blessing it, breaking it, and giving it out. The fact that Jesus *did not* stay long enough to eat anything in that story is rather extraordinary. Luke has an interest in showing that the resurrected Jesus had the kind of body that could eat. If the author of the gospel were making the stories up, there was ample opportunity to write Emmaus as a story in which Jesus ate.

Whaddya Want?

But perhaps the most significant display of ordinariness for our purposes comes earlier in the life of Jesus. There was a blind man begging on the road near Jericho. Hearing that Jesus was passing by, he called out to Jesus. "What do you want me to do for you?" Jesus asks.

Doesn't this strike you as kind of a stupid thing to ask? If I had been the blind guy, I know I would have squinted behind my dark glasses and brandished my white cane to punctuate my words: "What do you *think* I want, El Prophetismo? I'm blind!"

Now, alright. I know that probably very few blind people in the first century had white sticks, seeing-eye dogs, and dark glasses. But I find it difficult to believe that the man could walk or be led over to Jesus (Mark 10:50; Luke 18:40) without Jesus figuring out what was wrong with him. Jesus was perceptive enough to work out people's motivations before they spoke; he was perceptive enough to work out that he was dealing with a blind man.

Throughout the book, however, it has become clear that Jesus was usually plying the questions he asked for purposes *other* than the acquisition of knowledge. This is no exception. He wants the man to reply, but it is not data that he desires. This odd question stands directly in line with the central question of the gospels: "Who do you say that I am?" Like the parables, the questions are not about the answer as much as they are about the answerer. The questions, like the parables, force the people with whom Jesus is conversing to take a stand and make a decision. *That* is what he's after. He wants the blind man to declare himself. "Who touched me?" He wanted the woman to declare herself. "Who do you say that I am?" He wanted his followers to declare themselves. Jesus' questions in the gospels are like the "handshaking" that you hear when you connect a computer to a network using an old-fashioned modem. Beeeep ... scrrrraggggckkk ... zzzzzzzhhh ... ggggjjjjj. As my technically minded friend Brett saw best to explain it to me, that sound is the teensy little man that lives inside my modem asking and answering questions over the phone to the other little man who lives inside the computer on the other end. "I'm using this computer language, what language are you using? I can receive signals at this speed, how fast can you send it?" It is almost as if Jesus spoke Modem Language. He didn't *always* do miraculous spooky stuff, he didn't always tell stories, he didn't even always ask questions. But in everything he did and said was this element of modem handshaking. "I'm on this wavelength; what wavelength are you on?"

Something I've not mentioned up until now, really, is that the God of the Old Testament also appears as an asker of questions. There are questions to Moses, questions to kings, questions to prophets. The book of Jonah ends with God's question—a challenge to the prophet to change his attitude. To ancient Job's objections, he asks, essentially, Who do you think you are, Potshard-face? (Job 38:4). He too used questions to get at matters of relationship rather than information. Back in the very first book of the Bible, just after the Fall, when Adam and Eve try to escape from God's presence for the first time, God asks, "Where are you?" (Gen. 3:9) Jesus, in his day, was asking the same question. "Where are you?"

The Greatest Teacher?
We're now, at long last, in a position to answer my friend in the leather jacket, to evaluate Jesus: the greatest teacher

that ever lived or a failure? In the first chapter I tried to describe the greatest teacher in terms of ideal characteristics. And in some ways, Jesus didn't fit. The curious thing is that when instead of abstract ideals I try to think of the best teachers that I've actually known, they also don't fit. Bottomless depths of knowledge? Totally persuasive in argument? Nah. The thing that links them all was energy, passion, a slightly different and infectious way of looking at things, but most of all, an active interest in their students. They were the ones who interacted, who asked, who forced you to think, but allowed you to think for yourself.

Jesus, it seems, had no desire to become a great debater and convincer. What we said about the parables earlier was that they acted on fence-sitters like a sharp stick, forcing you one way or the other. The surprise is that throughout his teaching, Jesus didn't exert undue pressure on you to land on his side of the fence. He was not in the convincing business, he was in the provoking business. His goal seems to have been to present people with opportunities to choose—perhaps even to *force* people to choose. In this he was incredibly successful. In fact, it seems he was only too successful. The Sadducees and Pharisees as well as the disciples were forced into decision and forced into action—with terrible and tragic consequences: in some ways he *had* to be put to death. But I think they are right who said about Jesus, "He asked for it," or, "He brought it upon himself." He wanted people to choose— he refused to talk them into following him; refused to prove who or what he was. It's not because he felt that one answer was as good as another, but rather because an answer is not good unless it's a genuine answer.

He's handshaking, in order to open up the lines of communication. Jesus once apparently said that he wanted, demanded, that people become like little children if they wanted to follow him (Matt. 18:3). Well, he became like a little child as well. Most children go through a very particular and peculiar questioning stage, during which they seem to ask the question "Why?" over and over again. And they ask it about things they could not possibly have the least interest in or comprehension of. Ask any father who has found himself embroiled in the discussion of the differences between nuclear fission and fusion while daubing little pink noses in white sunscreen cream.

Why do children do this? The answer is very simple. They don't want the information. They don't want to talk about the issue; they just want to talk. They want the relationship. They are reveling in the fact that they can say something that makes you answer, and that they can come up with a reply that works no matter what you say or how little of it they understood. If ever there was a good metaphor for the mortal human praying to a divine being, this is it. And our guess has to be that God enjoys the whole process as much as an earthly parent does. We are beginning to talk on the right wavelength. It is the first dabbling at genuine interaction.

Jesus asks a lot of questions. But he doesn't ask primarily because he wants to acquire knowledge, nor does he ask to help people realize they already have the knowledge. He asks to help people realize where they stand; he asks questions in order to give an occasion for a reply, in order to initiate a conversation. What Jesus wanted to know—what Jesus was *dying* to know—was "Why do you call me good? Who do you say that I am?"

Questions for Reflection and Discussion

1. One of the things I wanted to do with this book was help folks be amazed at the "nonspooky" things that Jesus did. What is your favorite story of Jesus' questions and answers, and how have your views about it or about him changed?

2. I've only briefly mentioned some of the questions asked in the Old Testament. Are there others you can think of?

3. Traditional churches make a big deal over having a time of "confession"—confessing our sins before God. But of course, if there is a God, he doesn't need us to do that for his information any more than Jesus needed to ask the blind man what he wanted. Is there value in such "confession" then?

4. My basic premise in the book has been that Jesus is the best kind of great teacher: The kind that provoked people to take stands and become all they can be. Do you see this in Jesus now, or am I reading too much into the gospels?

Acknowledgments

I owe a huge debt of gratitude to my wife, Shanese, and children, Kathryn and Alistair, for their patience, understanding, and encouragement along the way. That the book was ever finished is due in no small measure to their support, encouragement, and patience.

Particular thanks are due to Steve Moody whose willingness to commit himself to reading the drafts of each chapter kept me committed to writing and rewriting them. Amy Boucher Pye, my editor at Zondervan, was everything anyone could ask of an editor: responsive, patient, critical, appreciative, honest, and have I mentioned patient and responsive? Brett Jordan and Helena Van Deroef also read every chapter and made lots of useful suggestions and corrections. I'd also like to express gratitude to Derek Tidball, the principal of LBC, Ken Benjamin, who did some research with me on the business of Jesus' questions, as well as my colleagues Steve Motyer, Robert Willoughby, Alison Le Cornu, and Antony Billington for their suggestions, friendship, and prayers.

All teachers and writers are conscious of the formative influence of the good things that they have read and been taught. I'd especially like to pay tribute to Howard Marshall, TT Howard, Lloyd Carr, Howard Kee, Paul Sampley, and Peter Kreeft, all of whom could find their influence in everything that I do, including this book. I hope they won't be too horrified. I stumbled upon an article by JB Torrance on "Questioning Jesus' Questions" and even the little I understood of it was inspirational.

Colin Brookes and Rachel Shorey hung in there with me over the years, providing me with a venue to try out these developing ideas and lavishing their encouragement. Thanks, folks. Thanks too to our House Group "family" and the Men's Breakfast crew, especially Trevor Crowley and Robert Stent.

If anything in the book makes anyone laugh, it probably comes from my hanging out too long with the Not Revd. Enough David Burd and Gary "the Kid" Shogren. I would also like to take this opportunity to state categorically that none of the stories or gags used here are borrowed from Mark Greene, no matter what he tells you.

Thanks to Bruce Cockburn, Phil Keaggy, Bill Mallonee, Paul Johnson, and especially Terry Taylor (here I am; there you are) for music and lyrics that helped keep me going, and to Steve Jobs and Jonathan Ive at Apple Computer for writers' tools that inspire and enliven rather than stifle and discourage.

Thanks and apologies to the real people whose names and personalities were exaggerated, adapted, and merged with other people's to make the book's characters "Mrs. Bayster" and "Mr. Davidovitch." Thanks too to Richie, who really did say that all those years ago.

Ethical and Aesthetic Environmental Impact Statement: No Microsoft products were used by the author in the composition of this book.

Subject?Index

Scripture?Index

We want to hear from you. Please send your comments about this book to us in care of the address below. Thank you.

GRAND RAPIDS, MICHIGAN 49530 USA

WWW.ZONDERVAN.COM